READING FOR REAL

Open University Press

English, Language, and Education series

General Editor: Anthony Adams
Lecturer in Education, University of Cambridge

This series is concerned with all aspects of language in education
from the primary school to the tertiary sector. Its authors are
experienced educators who examine both principles and practice of
English subject teaching and language across the curriculum in the
context of current educational and societal developments.

TITLES IN THE SERIES

Narrative and Argument
Richard Andrews (ed.)

Time for Drama
Roma Burgess and Pamela Gaudry

Computers and Literacy
Daniel Chandler and Stephen Marcus (eds.)

Readers, Texts, Teachers
Bill Corcoran and Emrys Evans (eds.)

Thinking Through English
Paddy Creber

Developing Response to Poetry
Patrick Dias and Michael Hayhoe

The Primary Language Book
Peter Dougill and Richard Knott

**Children Talk About Books: Seeing
Themselves as Readers**
Donald Fry

Literary Theory and English Teaching
Peter Griffith

Assessing English
Brian Johnston

**Lipservice: The Story of Talk in
Schools**
Pat Jones

**The English Department in a
Changing World**
Richard Knott

Oracy Matters
Margaret MacLure, Terry Phillips and
Andrew Wilkinson (eds.)

Beginning Writing
John Nichols *et al.*

Teaching Literature for Examinations
Robert Protherough

Developing Response to Fiction
Robert Protherough

**Microcomputers and the Language
Arts**
Brent Robinson

English Teaching from A–Z
Wayne Sawyer, Anthony Adams and
Ken Watson

Reconstructing 'A' Level English
Patrick Scott

Collaboration and Writing
Morag Styles (ed.)

**Reading Within and Beyond the
Classroom**
Dan Taverner

Reading for Real
Barrie Wade (ed.)

English Teaching in Perspective
Ken Watson

The Quality of Writing
Andrew Wilkinson

The Writing of Writing
Andrew Wilkinson (ed.)

Spoken English Illuminated
Andrew Wilkinson, Alan Davies and
Deborah Berrill

READING FOR REAL

EDITED BY
Barrie Wade

Open University Press
Milton Keynes · Philadelphia

Open University Press
Celtic Court
22 Ballmoor
Buckingham MK18 1XW

and

1900 Frost Road, Suite 101
Bristol, PA 19007, USA

First Published 1990
Reprinted 1990

British Library Cataloguing in Publication Data

Reading for real. – (English language, and education
  series)
  1. Great Britain. Schools.   Curriculum subjects:
  Reading Teaching
  I. Wade, Barrie, *1939–*   II. Series
  428.4′07′1041

  ISBN 0-335-09554-2 (paper)

Library of Congress Cataloging-in-Publication Data

Reading for real / edited by Barrie Wade.
       p.   cm.—(English, language, and education)
    Includes index.
    ISBN 0-335-09554-2
    1. Reading.   2. Reading—Parent participation.   3. Books and
  reading.   4. Reading readiness.   I. Wade, Barrie.   II. Series:
  English, language, and education series.
  LB1050.42.R43   1989   89-34767
  372.4—dc20   CIP

Typeset by Rowland Phototypesetting Limited
Bury St Edmunds, Suffolk
Printed in Great Britain by Biddles Limited
Guildford and King's Lynn

for
Jack Ousbey and Cliff Moon

Contents

Contributors

Muriel Bridge was trained at Homerton College, Cambridge and taught in primary schools in Norfolk, Warwickshire and Leicester. She retired recently after eighteen years service with the Leicestershire Literacy Support Service of which she was deputy head for the final five years. It was during this period that the literacy project 'Learning to Read' was undertaken. She is married with two daughters and five grandchildren.

Chris Burman has taught in primary schools for fourteen years. Most of her teaching experience has been with children in the 3–7 age range. In 1984, while studying for a Diploma in Professional Studies in Education in children's literature she began researching the role of literature in the development of literacy. Shortly afterwards she successfully implemented a 'real-book' approach in a Birmingham primary school. Chris is now an advisory teacher for English with Birmingham Education Support Service.

Valerie Cherrington has taught in primary and secondary schools and has been an advisory teacher on the Birmingham oracy project. She is now an advisory teacher for English with Birmingham Education Support Service.

Maura Fitzpatrick is headteacher at St Mary's RC Junior and Infant School, Harborne, Birmingham where she is engaged in developing school language policies which, in her own words, are relevant, purposeful and enjoyable.

Lena Strang is a teacher of English at Joseph Chamberlain Sixth Form College, Birmingham. She was born and educated in Finland and grew up as a Swedish and Finnish bilingual. She has taught English in a number of multi-ethnic secondary schools in the Midlands during the last fourteen years, including one year on teacher exchange in Jamaica.

Barrie Wade has taught in mainstream primary and secondary schools. He is senior lecturer in the University of Birmingham's School of Education, editor of *Educational Review* and is the author of a number of books on educational topics. He has also edited books for schools and published poetry, fiction and non-fiction for both children and adults.

Lynda Yard is the Croydon co-ordinator of the National Oracy Project. Previously she was an advisory teacher for language development and a primary school teacher.

Acknowledgements

Some of the material in Chapters 1, 2 and 6 is adapted from previously published articles by Barrie Wade: acknowledgements are made to the editors of *Cambridge Journal*, *Children's Literature in Education*, *English in Education*, *The West Midlands Journal of Teacher Education* and *Educational Review*.

Grateful thanks are given and acknowledgements made to the following for permission to quote copyright materials: to John Burningham and Jonathan Cape Ltd for the text from *The Snow* in the Little Books series; to Ladybird Books Ltd for the extract from *Things We Like* from the Key Words Reading Scheme. The extracts from *Rosie's Walk* (Pat Hutchins) and *Whistle for Willie* (Ezra Jack Keats) are reproduced by kind permission of The Bodley Head.

General editor's introduction

In his own introduction to this book Barrie Wade makes reference to some of the points about reading made by the National Curriculum's English Working Group. The original report of the Working Group identified two attainment targets for reading: one essentially concerned with reading for enjoyment, the other with reading for information. In its later comments on this report the National Curriculum Council has rejected this division as being too artificial and instead recommended a single attainment target for reading. This recognition of reading as unitary is very much within the spirit of Barrie Wade's book.

Two other main themes throughout this book seem to me also of paramount importance. The first is the recognition that much of reading is essentially a 'social' activity. Of course, in adult life we tend to read in conditions of relative solitude. It is one of the oddities of schooling, especially at the secondary level, that we expect 25 adolescents all to read the same book at the same time (and often, even, at the same pace). But even as adults we have a strong impulse to 'share' our reading, to borrow and lend books and to discuss our enjoyment of them with others. Much of the best (and worst) of traditional literary criticism has been born out of precisely this concept of 'sharing books together'. And recent work has shown the continuing importance of the shared story, either through reading aloud or through story telling. All this becomes even more important, of course, with the youngest children, who can be encouraged to enjoy stories even before they are able to read. Indeed, part of the motivation for learning to read at all (surely one of the most difficult learning tasks we ever carry out) is the recognition that those strange marks on paper that comprise print are a means of unlocking the exciting world of story.

All this is well documented in the opening chapters of this book and there is a welcome stress on reading as a collaborative activity which leads on naturally to the discussion in Chapter 7 of how older children can benefit in their writing of narrative by having a real (in this case younger) reader in mind. We are also publishing in this series a book edited by Morag Styles on *Collaboration and Writing*, which is in many ways complementary to the present volume. It approaches the same essential issues from a fundamentally not dissimilar standpoint but, as its title suggests, focuses upon these issues from the opposite end of the literacy task. To read both books together will be illuminating since they both draw our attention to the fundamental unity of all good language work. They point to the dangers of atomization that many fear may be one consequence of the testing procedures of the new National Curriculum in England and Wales. This concern with the essential unity of language across all four of its modes is the other major theme to spring off the page of the present work.

Chapter 9 demonstrates how such holistic attitudes to language can be combined with an essential rigour in monitoring and assessing individual progress. The developmental record proposed there can be easily and effectively used in the classroom and genuinely starts from the behaviour and learning patterns of the child, rather than seeking to impose some supposedly objective (and often arbitrary) framework within which assessment is supposed to take place. This chapter seems to me to make a real contribution to the current well-worn debate on assessment in English, again complemented by other books in this series, such as Don Fry's *Children Talk About Books* and Brian Johnston's *Assessing English*.

While this book was being written and edited a major controversy was taking place in the educational press over the extent to which teachers on an in-service course were being discouraged from using 'reading scheme' or 'basal readers' in their classrooms. In spite of the wide-ranging research evidence and the lack of money for school purchases, it is surprising how many such readers are still to be found in many schools and the extent to which some teachers are wedded to them. The present volume adopts a robust and characteristically uncompromising attitude on this issue – as its title indicates. The many references to 'real' books, suitable for a wide range of ages, will provide every experienced or beginning teacher with a wealth of new books to enjoy and old friends to be remembered. For this 'mature' reader at least, part of the pleasure of the present text has been seeing what other teachers and their students have made of books that I read long ago and which, in some cases, I had until now forgotten.

For me, as a secondary specialist in English, two of the most helpful texts on reading I have come across are both mentioned in the bibliography of this book. They are Vera Southgate's *Extending Beginning Reading* and Jesse F. Reid's *Learning to Think About Reading*, both classics of their kind. This volume follows in the tradition that they pioneered and seems to me likely to be equally helpful to a new generation of secondary, as well as primary, teachers, who are now facing the additional challenge of the National Curriculum.

ANTHONY ADAMS

Introduction

BARRIE WADE

The emphasis in this book is not only upon the discovery of meaning in purposeful acts of reading, but upon the sharing of those meanings for real purposes in a wider community. Interaction and sharing with others are fundamental to the process of becoming a reader at home, at school, in the workplace and in society at large. As Jerome Bruner (1986, p. 126) argues:

> Most learning in most settings is a communal activity, a sharing of the culture. It is not just that the child must make his knowledge his own, but that he must make it his own in a community of those who share his sense of belonging to a culture. It is this that leads me to emphasise not only discovery and invention but the importance of negotiating and sharing.

The five parts of the book encourage readers to explore their own experience of the process of reading and offer a good many practical suggestions for developing appropriate literacy environments for young readers. While the main focus is upon developing reading for 3–11 year olds, there are implications throughout for older students and Chapter 7, for example, explicitly deals with adolescents helping younger children to become readers.

Part One, 'Reading from home to school', confirms parents' active role in developing reading through reference to some research studies. The child at risk is the one whose parents do not point out print, do not tell stories and never read aloud. Reading is a shared, social activity, has purpose, gives pleasure and is linked to the other language modes of listening, talking and writing. Most children come to reading with a developed sense of story and oral abilities that can be built on, and with expectations of becoming literate. Parents and teachers have an important role in fostering a love of story and the fun of playing with language through talking with children and sharing and celebrating books. Methods of teaching frequently need re-examining and this first part explores the relevance and efficiency of time-honoured approaches, such as phonics or look-and-say, in relation to the needs of the young child developing in a community of readers. Reading is viewed holistically and emphasis is placed upon the experience of language that developing readers can draw upon – if they are allowed to. As the report of the National Curriculum English Working Group (DES 1988a, 9.7) says:

> Teachers should recognise that reading is a complex but unitary process and not a set of discrete skills which can be taught separately in turn and, ultimately, bolted together.

Part Two 'Reading: the first two key stages' is essentially practical and is intended to assist teachers who are developing a whole-language approach to reading in their classrooms and to provide encouragement for those wishing to embark on a literature-based approach to reading. Chapter 3 shows ways of organizing for success in reading in the early stages and in Chapter 4 Maura Fitzpatrick similarly explores the essentials for success with 7–11 year olds. Both chapters describe progress and practice in actual schools, thus providing ideas for teachers to utilize and develop in their own classrooms in programmes of study throughout the primary phases of education.

Part Three, 'Resources and support', provides a series of resources to help establish and support the theory and practice which have been outlined so far in the book. It is essential that reading is not seen merely as a school-based activity and Chris Burman shows how parents can be involved as active partners in developing readers from the beginning. Her chapter offers interesting examples of booklets which parents will find useful, as well as showing the advantages of reading logs. The other chapter in this part offers a series of practical strategies to develop and support readers and reading throughout the primary years. These will need to be adapted with reference to actual schools and individual children but they offer useful starting points. Similarly, the annotated booklists are meant to be a helpful resource to be modified and added to rather than utilized slavishly.

Part Four, 'Writing to read', emphasizes the connections between reading and writing as well as the listening and talking that goes on when children create books collaboratively. Writing and reading are different sides of the same coin: through writing books young people develop insight into how reading works for different audiences and for a variety of purposes. Lena Strang shows how her older students learned to construct narratives for younger readers and Valerie Cherrington describes the collaborative creation of a non-narrative text by young writers who came to understand how information books work for readers. It was C. Day Lewis who crystallized the exploratory function of writing when he said 'I write not to be understood, but to understand'. The writing of books certainly develops understanding and creates valid, interesting, home-produced reading materials and these chapters provide support for teachers wishing to develop similar understanding and competence in their own classrooms. It is important that young readers and writers see that they are going through the same processes as published writers and practised readers: '. . . it is important that pupils perceive that whenever they write they are sharing the medium with those whom they may regard as writers' (DES 1987, p.3).

Part Five, 'Assessing and monitoring progress', offers two contributions to the problem of how we evaluate progress in reading. In the mid-1970s the Bullock Report (DES, 1975) showed how invalid measures of reading age were. Virtually all the tests of reading abilities used today still measure them as discrete skills; further, they measure them in test situations, usually with decontextualized language. This kind of assessment is far removed from the situation of a young reader engaged in making meaning of a story or an information book. Lynda Yard shows how observations of young readers' behaviour can be used to record achievement and progress as part of normal classroom activities. Muriel Bridge discusses evidence from a county-wide longitudinal study of reading achievement which shows how effective a 'real-reading' approach is, especially in generating positive attitudes. There is little point in training children to read by forcing them to jump through the hoops of a reading scheme if, at the end of the training, they do not *want* to read. We are not in the business of teaching reading (I doubt if reading *can* be taught in a transactional way); rather we should be engaged in encouraging young people to become readers of books. Nothing is achieved if a child can read but chooses never to do so. This book provides a resource not merely to help children to read, but to help them to become readers.

PART ONE
Reading from home to school

1 Ready for reading

BARRIE WADE

Parent–teacher partnership

'What a pity Richard can read', said the headmistress. 'He's going to miss so much in the infant school.' What vistas of concern suddenly open – in an interview to discuss a child's entry to school – for teacher and parent! The headteacher, having decided on the Initial Teaching Alphabet ten years previously as the medium for teaching reading, and having decided on a particular reading scheme, has the prospect of coping with a child who can already competently read the last book in that scheme in traditional orthography. For Richard's mother a whole enjoyable retrospect of endless talking, bedtime stories, tracing, labelled drawings and printed accounts of bluebell-picking trips pasted in the kitchen is suddenly illuminated by a flash of guilt. She can also see (wrongly, maybe) Richard bored and unoccupied while 33 other infants together chant 'mei bwk'. No. She will not mention that he can also *write*. Richard meanwhile has the clear, unfocused eyes of the nearly 5 year old who knows that adults occasionally talk as if he were not there and is unaware that he has recently become a problem. Such are the perils of not conforming to expectations! We may know that individuals develop at different rates, have different experiences and different abilities but when education is systematized the convenience of treating everyone alike becomes dangerously attractive.

It is not only the 'system', the problem of coping with large numbers of children in reception classes, or even the lack of nursery provision in many areas, which reinforces this attitude. Even some of the better work in developmental psychology has occasionally led to misinterpretation. To take one example: Gesell *et al*. (1977) have described the cycle of development in seven stages (Shakespeare's seven ages?) but warn against interpreting these growth gradients as statistical age norms. None the less, 'for convenience', these gradients and maturing traits are arranged in levels to which *precise ages* are attached. It is this 'convenience' which often leads to misunderstanding.

More than a decade later the Secretary of State for Education and the

Secretary of State for Wales gave terms of reference to the Cox Committee which defined attainment targets as

> clear objectives for the knowledge, skills, understanding and aptitudes which pupils of different abilities and maturity should be expected to have acquired *at or near certain ages.*

DES 1988a, 1.2, added italics

They were clearly looking for norms such as that which Gesell *et al.* (1977) give for a 5 year old:

> Much of FIVE's reading and number work is closely associated with his play, both at home and at school. He can pick out capital letters, first at the left, or right of a page and then at the beginning of a sentence in the text. Later he reads letters in combination, such as 'C - A - T' and asks what they spell.

It is perhaps natural to see a prescription in this kind of text. Even if a parent or teacher recognizes that this is meant to be *descriptive* she or he also needs to remember that some 5 year olds will be achieving a great deal more and (since Gesell's clinical work was done with children of 'high-average and superior' intelligence from homes of 'good or high socio-economic status') some a great deal less. More serious, though, is the assumption that there is *one single way* in which children start and progress in their reading from capital letters to groups of capital letters. This may indeed be one of the least helpful ways to begin since the sounds 'C' (See) 'A' (Ay) 'T' (Tee), separately or together, do not remotely resemble 'cat'.

We remember that in another publication, *English 5–16* (DES 1984), the first reading objective given for 16 year olds was that they should 'read whole books of some length requiring some persistence'. Until that time many children were presumably expected to acquire the separate skills of reading incrementally, to cobble them together and prepare for whole books in later adolescence! This simplistic ladder model of reading development bears little resemblance to the reality of how children do learn to become readers.

The plain fact is that many children actually read whole stories, words and sentences *before* they understand the relationship between letters. The facts about how individual children learn to read cannot be contained in one single theory. The notions of 'growth' and 'development' cannot be applied directly to reading as if it were a naturally acquired process (though a thoughtful teacher or parent might make it appear natural). It is a mistake to look for 'readiness' as if it were some outward sign or visible signal, magically appearing to say, 'It's now safe to start him on Book 1'. The child is more than a marrow growing in a garden, watched over but fed twice only at different stages of its development. Parent and teacher frequently need to intervene in the learning process. Readiness for reading can be encouraged as well as waited for and is not quite the same as being 'ready' for a first haircut or 'ready' for the next size in shoes.

Normal children acquire the structures of their spoken language naturally and they extend their abilities by putting their language to use for a variety of purposes. This acquisition, experimentation and practice goes on through most of the young child's waking hours, particularly if adults are willing to engage in conversation. However, children may not, of course, be *surrounded* by print in quite the same natural way. Nor can they practise by themselves until they have mastered some of the requirements of the writing system. Further, they are dealing with a more abstract system than speech. They have learned that the sound 'dog' represents the barking reality, but they also have to learn that the letters 'd-o-g' together represent both the sound and that reality. Most children learning this process will need systematic help and sustaining over a fairly long period. But there is nothing to suggest that this help should suddenly begin at the 'rough-and-readiness' age of 5 and in school. This is as likely to isolate reading from other activities and from the home. A child who has seen no one reading for five years is likely to find the sudden stress on it at school disconcerting. Just as reading does not necessarily *begin* in the infant school, so it does not end there either. Reading is not something to be left alone, once acquired, like the ability to use a knife and fork. Junior, middle and secondary teachers have the job of leading a child into understanding of reading for different purposes (scanning, skimming, studying, etc.) and coping with the various demands of specialist school subjects. In these tasks a parent also has a continuing, supporting role to play.

Children mature at different rates and the reading process is an individual one; but the child who has been fortunate in having an encouraging environment with considerable opportunity for spontaneous learning will have a head start. When early readers have been compared with groups who learned later, the early readers were usually well ahead even after several years of schooling. The significant factor may be the help given by parents. John Hughes (1975) reports one American study where all the early readers had been helped by parents, while the general attitude of parents of the slower readers was that reading should be taught by a teacher in school.

There is a growing body of research into the links between practices of child rearing in the home and educational achievement in the school, though the findings on what kind of home environment leads to educational success are not clear cut. One study (Kent and Davis 1975) suggested that the best kind of home was one where high standards were set from an early age and where rewards were infrequent and conditional upon achievement. Another, (Fraser 1959), found that a 'democratic', friendly and spontaneous environment was most effective. Perhaps the main implication from these reports is that no study suggests that a *laissez-faire*, wait-and-see, non-intervening environment is helpful to educational success. When reading specifically is considered, research evidence seems to point in a similar direction. A study of 1,544 children aged 7–9 (Clark 1970) showed that a lack of parental help was one of the important factors adversely affecting the ability to read.

There have been many studies of children who are failing or finding the going hard in reading; but fewer have looked carefully enough at able readers and at the factors contributing to their success. Margaret Clark (1976) studied fluent readers to determine why it is that some children develop higher-order reading skills early on. Her results suggest that the process does not depend so much on IQ as upon such factors as the quality of language interaction between parents and children; whether books are brought to the children's attention, discussed with them and whether they have pictures and print pointed out; whether they have older brothers and sisters who can and do read in the home.

These studies suggest that the child who learns to read early will have an advantage not only in earlier development of a skill but also in early access to the world of information and pleasure that reading brings. This advantage may be of most value to the slow-learning child. On the other hand, if children are given little or no encouragement to put experiences into words, if stories and books are not part of their natural world and if they are not shown the significance of letters and words even when they show interest, their difficulties can only be compounded and the school's task can become very difficult indeed.

The evidence should not be wrongly interpreted to indicate an unhealthy return to the dangerous practice of putting inordinate pressure upon infants to succeed at a level beyond their capabilities. However, both schools and parents can take positive support from these studies for an active partnership role in helping a child's developing reading abilities. Innate potential and home background – in the sense of father's occupation and the amount of schooling parents had – seem to be less important than was once thought. More seems to depend on the availability of interested people to talk with children, to read to them, to answer their questions and to stimulate their interest in books and libraries.

Story is a powerful tool. Shirley Brice Heath (1982, 1983) verifies that an awareness of story helps children into reading. Those children who have this awareness from stories that have been read or told to them become those who enjoy reading and willingly do it. Gordon Wells (1982) found that the greatest indicator of reading success after two years at school was the knowledge of the conventions of reading possessed by the child at entry to school, which, in turn, was strongly predicted by the frequency of stories read at home. So parents have a crucial part to play.

To summarize: the argument here is that, though there are differences between reading and other modes of language use, too much has been made of the school's *unaided* role in beginning and developing reading. If parents have lost confidence in their ability to help children, preferring 'not to interfere', then that is not in the best interests of their children. When reading is treated as a mystique, then schools, parents and the relationship between them all suffer. Schools cut themselves off from a tremendous, untapped resource in developing reading abilities – parents. Schools can play a valuable role in enlisting this aid by giving parents the confidence to help and more specific directions about what to do. Awareness of this partnership in responsibility is likely to lead to changes in attitudes to teaching reading and to the system accommodating itself to individual differences.

The three Rs: rhyme, rhythm and repetition

Parents and teachers seek to foster and extend the language abilities of individual children in appropriate ways. It is becoming accepted, for example, that reading takes place in a context which influences the reading process and is not merely a skill to be practised in isolation. An adult taking this view of reading is likely to draw upon a child's oral abilities in a 'language experience' approach. As well as talk, other language from a child's environment – such as shopping lists, recipes, destinations on buses and print from sauce bottles or cereal packets – may be used to build upon abilities already present and to make links between oral and literary modes of language. In casting widely for learning experiences and materials a teacher is more likely to communicate that reading can be both enjoyable and useful. The variety and validity that pupils perceive in such materials is also likely to sustain interest and motivation.

A similarly convincing argument can be put forward for the value of links between spoken language and literature. Since some stories are told orally the connections are made directly apparent. The young child who is told nursery rhymes at home and school is led into an imaginative world, a world of oral poetry that lays important foundations for later language work. The child with a rich oral language experience is well set up to cope with the abstract quality of written language which, as Vygotsky (1962) says, forms a stumbling block for many language learners.

Let us take one rhyme to illustrate five of the qualities which make such material valuable.

> One finger, one thumb keep moving,
> One finger, one thumb keep moving,
> One finger, one thumb keep moving,
> We'll all be merry and bright.

This little rhyme is above all simple and direct; secondly, it is rhythmic and uses the tunes of speech; thirdly, it is repetitive, giving practice and pleasure in savouring the words and their sounds. Fourthly, the rhyme is meant to be acted out by the child:

> One finger, one thumb, one arm, one leg,
> One nod of the head, keep moving . . .

and in participating in these actions and saying the rhyme the child is instrumental in linking language and action. Fifthly, the rhyme in its simple narrative progression provides a linked sequence of predictable units that have meaning and are worth repeating. Learning that language is predictable helps develop the anticipation which plays an important role in both reading and understanding narratives.

These five advantages, then, are useful in developing a child's concept of story. They are also useful in making links between speech and written-down language. Most of the well known rhymes are themselves simple stories. 'Sing a song of sixpence', for example, has a clearly defined setting and episode structure, with the maid having her nose pecked off after setting a 'dainty dish' before the king. Such rhymes and songs use a narrative framework and, through pleasurable contact with these frameworks, a child's notion of what a story is develops. There are, of course, many hundreds of traditional rhymes and jingles which children listen to and chant, so developing not only their abilities to feel and use the sounds and rhythms of spoken language, but also their understanding of what story is.

Rhymes and jingles share another important attribute with stories: they not only tell of the real world but also extend reality imaginatively. Rhymes frequently provide information about the natural world.

> The leaves are green, the nuts are brown
> They hang so high they won't come down;
> Leave them alone till frosty weather,
> Then they will all come down together.

Sometimes they inform about specific events, as in the grim commentary on bubonic plague:

> Ring-a-ring o' roses
> A pocket full of posies.
> A-tishoo! A-tishoo!
> We all fall down.

Interestingly, though, information seems to matter less than the pleasure children take in sounds, rhythms and actions and in the whole structure of the rhyme. Of course, children may learn some concepts from rhymes; but that is not the main or only reason for introducing them. A grasp of the concepts 'up' and 'down' may be obtained from 'The grand old Duke of York', but a child can also savour the marching rhythm and the splendid purposelessness of aristocratic action for its own sake. Few children ask what a 'muffin man' is or where 'Drury Lane' is while they listen to the rhyme or chant it to a blindfolding game. There are many adults who would have difficulty identifying a mulberry bush, though they went round one often enough in their childhood play! Why a mulberry bush? Why go round it? And why on a cold and frosty morning? These are unimportant questions not because answers could not be provided to them: they are unimportant because no child ever asks them.

In rhymes and more developed stories reality is extended imaginatively and children quickly learn that stories do not work at a merely literal level. In the real world nutmegs and pears do not grow upon the same tree, but a rhyme and a story have their own logic and appeal to feelings and imagination rather than being rational and empirical. This appeal is apparent in the majority of rhymes.

> There was a man lived in the moon,
> Lived in the moon, lived in the moon,
> There was a man lived in the moon,
> And his name was Aiken Drum
> And he played upon a ladle,

A ladle, a ladle,
And he played upon a ladle,
And his name was Aiken Drum.

The imaginative extension in rhymes such as these is all important; the narrative is shaped and elaborated for its own sake. Part of the magic and imaginative awakening lies in the sounds of words and their arrangement (noticeable in names like Aiken Drum). Incy Wincy Spider and Rumpelstiltskin have for young children the imaginative stimulus that names like 'Chimborazo, Cotopaxi and shining Popocatapetl' provided for Walter James Turner.

The child who included Turner's poem in Kaye Webb's (1979) collection of verse chosen by children gave as the reason 'it's so dream-like and I don't know the meaning of two or three words which makes it all the more secretish. It's the favourite of my favourite poems.' Rhymes and stories, like good poetry, can be appreciated before they can be understood. Seamus Heaney (1980) tells of his own childhood experience of words on radios – words like Hilversum, Leipzig and Droitwich – and of the powerful impact of strange words in the catechism or in the 'enforced poetry' of prayer or the 'sprung rhythm' of the shipping forecast. Dogger Bank, Fair Isle and Channel Light Vessel are names which can fire the imagination. Heaney talks of these early contacts with names as 'bedding the ear' with a linguistic hardcore that can some day be built on. His account is valuable in suggesting that childhood contacts with stirring, imaginative words and the maturely organized verse of the adult are part of the same continuum. These words may be in unlikely places, like those South Wales place names on the sides of railway coal trucks which stirred the imagination of J. R. R. Tolkien when he was a boy: names like Nantyglo, Senghenydd, Blaen-Rhondda, Penrhiwceiber and Tredegar which he 'did not know how to pronounce but which had a strange appeal to him' (Carpenter 1977, p.26). We need to remember that although rhymes contain many examples of imaginative language they are not the exclusive source.

Part of the learning which a child intuitively absorbs in rhymes like 'Aiken Drum' is that language is also used for imaginative purposes as well as for trans-actions in the literal world of reality. Rhymes encourage the playing with language which begins with an infant reproducing sounds for fun and which is also much in evidence in children's love of riddles, puns and language jokes of all kinds.

Why do dragons sleep in the daytime?
Because they like to hunt knights.

What did the spaceman see in the frying pan?
An unidentified frying object.

Knock Knock!
Who's there?
Cows go.
Cows go who?
No, cows go 'moo' not 'who'.

It is not only children with a sophisticated command of language who derive this kind of pleasure. One seven year old in an educational assessment unit recently spent a good deal of one particular day repeating with obvious pleasure a rhyme his mother had taught him the day before:

> Twinkle twinkle little star
> What you say is what you are.

Natural enthusiasm for this kind of verbal play can be used to good effect when a child has begun reading. Indeed, a love of language for its own sake and pleasure in playing with language link the world of children's rhyme with the world of adult fiction and poetry.

It is worthwhile, then, to foster and extend children's pleasure in words, jingles, jokes and riddles, bearing in mind that, as the Bullock Committee note (DES 1975, 5.20):

> it is a remarkable fact that infants have the vocabulary, if not the concepts, of the technological, polluted, divided world that television presents to them.

Television has the advantage of presenting to children a complex range of language. Vocabulary, accents, registers, intonation patterns and dialects become available in a variety which would not otherwise be possible. It is as well to remember this advantage while examining the influence of TV rhymes and jingles. Otherwise some teachers' pejorative view of television's influence may prejudice a proper evaluation. A primary school pupil was recently engaged on an exercise which asked her to use individual words in sentences. One of the words was 'judicious'. She wrote 'Hands that judicious can be soft as your face', which is how she had heard the TV jingle advertisement for a well-known washing up liquid.

It is possible to mock the child's misunderstanding and the TV medium without also noticing the fatuity of the school exercise that the child is engaged in. The 'wrong' language had at least been learned in a context where the visual information of a glamorous woman 'doing dishes' accompanied the language; in school the child was asked to use bits of language out of context and unrelated to any of the ways in which language is normally used.

Generalizations about television are impossible to make since there is, for example, a vast difference between the experience of a child whose parent uses TV as a baby minder and that of a child whose parent selects programmes, also watches and talks over the programmes with the child. Television is neither good nor bad in itself; it all depends on how it is used.

This complexity is revealed in studies which attempt to investigate television watching in relation to reading stories. Frank Whitehead's national survey of children's reading interests (1974) failed to discover a simple relationship where TV watching took the place of reading. While some 'displacement' occurred, there were substantial numbers of pupils who watched a good deal of television and read many books; there were also substantial numbers who did neither. The fact is that television can stimulate children to read as well as taking up large quantities of their leisure time. It is clearly a mistake to assume that, if children normally spending, say, three hours a day watching TV were suddenly to stop, they would spend all that time (or any of it) reading books.

Attitudes to advertising also influence the judgements we make about commercial television. It is, of course, no accident that jelly babies are advertised just at the time when 3 and 4 year olds are sitting down to lunch or that baked beans and breakfast cereals bombard schoolchildren at tea-time. On the other hand, we have with luck left behind the simple view that all advertising is devious, pernicious and corrupting. Again, much depends on how it is used. Television advertising can be informative, entertaining and amusing, while admittedly it can also be blatant, irritating and contrived. Some people who have enjoyed the skill and humour of advertisements for, say, Guinness or Hamlet cigars have never felt the urge to drink or smoke.

When we consider advertising jingles, moral arguments frequently impinge upon the practical or utilitarian ones. An example is provided by Elaine Moss (1978) in her rejection of such material for story telling on the following grounds (p. 64):

> The adman's language is fine for advertisements. Just occasionally it is original, even brilliant. But as a language for enrichment of life, as a means for expressing complex thought it is sterile.

I have some sympathy with this view, although it remains true that the language of many children's books, particularly their 'reading books', is not suited to enrichment or complex expression either. It is true, as Elaine Moss says, that 'children in the reception class are less likely to know Wee Willie Winkie than the latest jingle ad. for Heinz Baked Beans' (p.64). However, this is no reason for excluding from classrooms any part of the oral experience which children bring with them. The argument confuses the re-creation and regeneration of language (to which advertising seldom contributes) with young children's need to practise rhythms and rhymes in their mother tongue and to gain pleasure from the sounds of words for their own sake. This latter aim links directly with the satisfactions to be found later in the contemplation of words and their arrangement in poetry. 'Beanz Meanz Heinz' and 'The murmurous haunt of flies on summer eves' may have more in common than the 'z' sounds. The skilled teacher may be able to use the knowledge of and pleasure in the first to lead to appreciation of the satisfaction in the second. So in the reception class it is first of all important to value *all* those areas where children have already absorbed narratives and taken pleasure in words, whether they are anecdotes, jingles, rhymes, folk tales, jokes or games. Secondly, it is important educational practice to promote further learning and to extend the knowledge, skills and pleasures that are embryonic in the young child.

If a pupil comes to school with no experience of TV jingles this is no guarantee that the parents will have taught the child 'Wee Willie Winkie'. The relationship between television and speech is as complex as that between TV and reading. Fortunately, most children do reach school with a knowledge of jingles, rhymes and stories although they may not be the ones that the teacher favours – or even knows. It is worth exploring the oral culture of children with a view to building on what concepts and abilities learners already have.

The central importance of story

Material collected by Iona and Peter Opie (1959) is abundant evidence of the way the culture of childhood is firmly embedded in an oral tradition. Children pass the traditions on to each other in language or games which are structured by language. The Opies have shown the central importance to children in all geographical areas of such things as truce terms, names or even predictions based on bus ticket numbers, for example. Their evidence of individual word-use suggests that one term is invariably in common usage in a given school, although the terms may vary from school to school or area to area. So in different places, children who want a temporary truce or a breather in a game may have to call 'kings', 'faynights', 'exes', 'cruses', 'pax', 'creams', 'cross kings', 'barley' or 'fingers'. The call is frequently reinforced non-verbally by a sign such as crossing fingers, to which some of the preceding terms make direct reference. We see here the way that language used by children in their peer group is naturally linked to action. Further, as the Opies say, children's use of language reflects two apparently conflicting elements – their respect for tradition and their love of fun.

These elements can perhaps be seen best in the more extended uses of language in clapping and skipping games. The following examples were collected in a single summer day with children from one British primary school, aged 5–11, occupied in their games during morning, afternoon and lunch-time breaks. It is likely that any school will reveal similar trends in usage to any unobtrusive observer.

Jumping games

A small group of children play a forfeit game involving one jumping and landing with legs apart or criss-crossed alternately on each syllable of a verse chanted by the rest:

> The cat's got the measles
> The measles
> The measles
> The cat's got the measles
> The measles got the cat

On the final syllable of the ironic ending, if a child lands with legs crossed, a forfeit (such as a shoe or sock taken off) is required.

Three children with a loop of elastic about two metres long play a more complex game. Two stand facing each other with the loop just tautened around their ankles. Then the third goes through a series of jumping manoeuvres using the two lines of elastic to make criss-cross shapes ('diamonds'), landing with both feet on the lines ('linesies') or twisting feet in the lines and jumping out cleanly ('twisties'). The simplest refrain used combines the traditional and fun elements that the Opies describe:

> England Ireland Scotland Wales
> Insies outsies twisties insies

Such chants feature both pattern and sequence and sometimes make little narratives – as when the measles polish off the cat.

Skipping games

The use of embryonic stories is more evident in the rhymes used for skipping games.

> Johnny Morgan plays the organ
> Jimmy played the drum
> His sister played the tambourine
> Till father smacked her bum

Narrative is frequently used to structure and guide action and in particular to provide a framework for turn taking. The stories may have traditional themes like stitching or more modern ones like cars. Here are three examples with accompanying actions.

Katie in the kitchen	*(Two children turn the rope while one skips)*
Doing a bit of stitching	
In comes the Bogie Man	*(Another child enters skipping)*
And out goes Katie	*(The first skipper departs)*
I had a little bumper car	*(One child enters turning rope and skips)*
A number 48	
I took it round the corner	*(He/she jumps out and runs round one of those holding the rope)*
And slammed on the brake	*(Then re-enters rope, skips, and finishes legs astride rope and stops it turning)*
Vote vote vote for Eliza Dickenson	*(Eliza skips)*
In comes Sally at the door	*(Sally joins Eliza)*
Eliza is a silly fool	
She fell into the lily pool	
We don't want her any more	
Chuck her out	*(Eliza leaves Sally skipping alone)*

In the next example, the story is even more extended as each verse develops the traditional theme of courtship, marriage and family, interwoven with twentieth-century concepts of Hollywood, picture going and register office weddings.

All the boys in Hollywood	
Aren't very nice	
Except for [Paul]	*(Any favourite boy's name)*
And he's all right	
He took me to the pictures	
Sat me on his knee	
And said, 'Oh darling	
Won't you marry me?'	
Yes, no, yes, no, yes . . .	*(Continues until skipper faults)*
How many kisses did he give you?	
100, 200, 300, 400 . . .	*(Continues until skipper faults)*
Where did you marry him	
Office, church, office, church . . .	*(Continues, etc.)*
How many children did he give you?	
1, 2, 3, 4 . . .	*(Continues until skipper faults)*

It is, of course, a simple matter to make the story appropriate to a boy skipper (as happened once) by changing minor elements.

Clapping games

Stories containing repetition, a fixed rhythm and counting are clearly appropriate to skipping games, but those children without a rope are not at a loss. Of the four clapping games being played this particular day, only two were recorded, but they provide evidence of further uses of story. Not only are there fixed rhythms and repetitions but appropriate actions fitted to the words (as in skipping games); each game also makes use of the traditional elemental story, birth–marriage–death, but gives it special additions. The first game, played with gusto, introduces an element of conflict to be resolved by the partners before marriage. The first two verses are:

I'm a little Dutch girl	*(No 1 skips up to partner and retires)*
Dutch girl, Dutch girl,	
I'm a little Dutch girl	*(No 1 repeats)*
Far from the sea	
I'm a little Dutch boy	*(No 2 skips up to partner and retires)*
Dutch boy, Dutch boy	
I'm a little Dutch boy	*(No 2 repeats)*
Far from the sea	

This verse pattern, skipping and turn taking continues with the following verses, some of which include additional actions.

Go away I hate you . . .	
Why do you hate me . . .	
Because you stole my necklace . . .	
Here's your dirty necklace . . .	*(No 2 also slaps partner's hands)*
Now we're getting married . . .	*(They also swing each other round)*

Now we're getting older . . .   *(They walk round each other slowly)*
Now we are dying . . .   *(They collapse slowly and lie down)*

The second example hardly bears thinking of in terms of the five ages of woman – the roles are so stereotyped – though it spans birth to old age deliberately. Interestingly, it was played by a girls-only group with ages ranging from 6 to 9.

As well as the clapping on all other lines, this story includes a mime on the last one of each verse, which is also spoken with appropriate tone and emphasis.

When Suzie was a baby
A baby Suzie was
And all she ever said to me
Was, 'goo, goo, a-goo, goo goo'.   *(Mime with thumb in mouth)*

When Suzie was a schoolgirl
A schoolgirl Suzie was
And all she ever said to me
Was, 'Hey, Miss. I can't do this.'   *(Mime with hand up)*

When Suzie was a teenager
A teenager she was
And all she ever said to me
Was, 'Ooh, Aah. I lost my bra.   *(Mime with raised eyebrows*
I left my knickers in my boyfriend's car.'   *and arms across chest)*

When Suzie was a mother
A mother Suzie was
And all she ever said to me
Was, 'Hey, Fred. Get out-er that bed.'   *(Mime with wagging finger)*

When Suzie was a granny
A granny Suzie was
And all she ever said to me
Was, 'knit, knit, a-knit, knit, knit'.   *(Mime knitting)*

From this examination of three kinds of game it is clear that story is an important way in which children transmit their cultures. The oral traditions are mediated as embryonic or more developed narratives, which are used to structure games. Story is therefore a natural part of children's experience, is strongly associated with pleasure and gives satisfaction through its capacity to shape and order.

The inventive and imaginative aspects of story are also evident both in adaptations and additions to traditional structures as well as in tag games like 'Poison'. In this, the child who is 'it' holds out her hands and the others each grab a finger or thumb and hold on to it while 'it' makes up a story aloud. The story she tells contains the word poison twice in the narrative. However, at the third mention of poison in the story, 'it' is allowed to tag one of the others if she can. Then that person stands in front, with the rest lined up in front of him. They all shout 'poison, poison, poison', run to grab his fingers and the game starts again. Considerable skills can be exercised in developing a narrative and children quickly become adept at embedding the key word naturally in their story to give them the best chance of catching an audience member unprepared.

Several points emerge from this brief examination of a small sample of the narratives children use naturally in their play. The texts of these stories are meaningful, structured and pleasure giving. Their language is linked to action and experience and their rhythms and repetitions are those of spoken language. 'Hop, hop hop to the golliwog shop', from a hopping game, may seem similar to 'See Spot. Run. Spot. Run', from a reading scheme, but the resemblance is superficial: children actually say the first; no child would say the second except when reading aloud from a scheme.

This examination of children's oral development shows the potential of anecdote, experience and the repetition and rhythms of structured games for learning reading. It is folly not to build upon the experience of language that children have already acquired in such a natural way. Paul Goodman (1974), tongue-in-cheek, says:

> We do not know scientifically how children learn to speak, but almost all succeed equally well . . . If we tried to teach children to speak, by academic methods in a school-like environment, many would fail and most would stammer.

Yet this is exactly how reading has been taught for decades and often in isolation from other modes of language. It is small wonder that many children failed and many 'stammered'. Some who learned to read never became voluntary and interested readers of books.

Knowledge of children's oral culture can help to develop useful starting points for schools and effective teaching strategies like:

- valuing and fostering what oral abilities children bring with them to school.
- being prepared to learn from children who can contribute appropriate material from another culture or even from another language.
- observing and drawing upon the rhymes and stories that children naturally use in their play and games, as well as those that are available in popular culture.
- encouraging participation in a wider range of rhymes and stories.
- using rhymes to give pleasure in themselves and also as material for other classroom activities such as reading.

Rhymes contribute to children's concepts of story and to their pleasure in language itself. There is every reason to make them an important part of early classroom activities. If we consider reading alone a sufficient case has been made, since meaning and pleasure in narrative are central to the act of reading itself – much more so than the pseudo-scientific, complex hierarchies of skills and sub-skills that have dominated past accounts of reading. The Bullock Committee (DES 1975) report that adult illiterates consistently say that they never realized that reading was an activity that other people engaged in for pleasure.

From the very beginning we need to establish the links between experience, speech and the written-down word. Celebrating and sharing meaningful stories and rhymes will do more for learners than will barren readiness exercises and reading schemes that do not seem to relate to the real world. We can teach children to jump through hoops, but we must not complain if they choose to do it passively or unresponsively. Children know the difference between real reading and words artificially arranged to teach reading. We remember the young child who was asked by his teacher to pass her a book. 'That's not a book', he said. 'That's a reading book.'

2 Approaches to reading

BARRIE WADE

However the reading process may be defined, whether as decoding print, piecing out meaning or as a 'reduction of uncertainty' (see Smith 1978b), it has been widely held by the teaching profession that a major emphasis should be placed upon teaching children to read. Many thousands of articles and hundreds of books have testified to the centrality of this aim. The disadvantages to a child of either pressure or neglect and of professional narrowness are perhaps obvious and have been explored in Chapter 1. The centrality of any objective should not mean that all others disappear from view. Children are complex beings and their needs cannot be neatly pigeon-holed, much less centrally channelled. We recognize, for example, that children need sleep, food, drink and shelter for healthy development. But we have also learned that it is best wherever possible to avoid keeping them permanently in institutions! Many studies show (e.g. Skeels 1966) that a further complex of needs – including attention, security and affection in interpersonal relationships – enable the young to thrive. Children lacking such sustenance have a much more difficult task.

It is certainly not easy to locate children with emotional and intellectual deficiencies. It is, however, part of the teacher's task to be a trained and perceptive observer and to intervene positively wherever possible to ensure healthy emotional and mental growth and adjustment. No one would dream of helping a starving child by feeding him or her on slimming biscuits. Yet if a teacher overemphasizes some aims to the exclusion of others, she/he must very carefully consider whether the actual learning experiences offered are so drained of life-giving substance that the child is subjected to an involuntary slimming down of already impoverished cognitive powers and already reduced affective strengths. It is also sad that later, when the training pressure to read is removed, many children seem to join a reading hunger strike. Frank Whitehead (1977), in a large scale survey of nearly 8,000 pupils' reading preferences, showed that from age 10 to age 14 the average number of books read per month declined from 3 to 1.9. More disturbing, and hidden by this general statistic, is the fact that the proportion of pupils who read nothing at all increased from 13 per cent at 10 to 36 per cent at 14.

The causes of this decline are certainly likely to be complex, but it looks as if many children (over one-third of all abilities) arrive at adolescence with the *ability* to read *but with no desire to do so*. Whatever the complexity of causes it seems that a certain amount of blame must be apportioned to schools which teach reading as a skill divorced from its purposes of pleasure and power. Whitehead's results showed links between the amount children read and the kind of schools they attended. For example, ten year olds in streamed classes read less than those in unstreamed classes and pupils in separate junior schools read less than those in mixed infant–junior schools. However, it is unsafe to proceed from correlations to causation. It may be that children read more where there is more continuity in reading policy and where there is less emphasis upon strictly cognitive, academic objectives. However, many other factors in the relationship between teachers and pupils certainly influence reading. Some of these (say, how often a pupil sees a teacher reading or how a teacher advises pupils about choosing books) are hard to measure, but may be more influential than type of school or organization.

The problem stemming from the kind of awareness discussed in the last paragraph is that a teacher may feel that since there are likely to be deficiencies anyway in some children's voluntary reading as they approach adolescence there is all the more reason to hammer reading into children before they become obdurate or capable of resistance! A problem with many surveys is that their results can become received wisdom and therefore self-fulfilling. In the recent past many primary teachers felt they could do little about anti-reading pressure from adolescents' peer groups or parents (Bardgett 1977), boring reading materials in secondary schools (Harrison 1979) or the competition from television and other pursuits (Whitehead *et al.* 1974) – causes which various writers have adduced to explain reluctance to read. But there is a good deal that primary teachers can do to make sure that their knowledge of children's books and of children's feelings about book reading complements a clear understanding of the processes of teaching reading.

Let us try to illustrate this by reference to some real children and real books, remembering how children frequently distinguish between 'real' books and 'reading' books and remembering too that reading schemes and policies require adaptation to the needs of individual readers.

First, let us examine the views of four children about reading, remembering that while they are honest views they are meant to be illustrative and not conclusive evidence.

1 *Michael* (6). I like reading / but Mrs R— don't she says you come and / read to me and then she starts shouting again.

According to Michael's teacher, he is most reluctant to read and frequently 'loses' his reading book. He is 'not very bright'.

Michael's teacher would no doubt be surprised (if she asked him) to discover that he liked reading. He would probably not have disclosed that it was her own verbal 'thump and say' method which upset him and which led him to believe that *she* did not like reading. However, she might have discovered enough about Michael's real feelings and attitudes to prompt a review and change of her approach and own attitude.

> 2 *Dean* (5): I like reading and football and I like writing best and Mrs H— reads us some stories / um / every day / well nearly every day / she lets us join in and / we all say some of it / it's good.

Dean's teacher claims little credit for his development in reading. Now in his second term at infant school, he came 'reading fluently' as a 'rising five' and his mother who had moved as a girl to Britain from Jamaica had apologized for 'teaching' him.

However, Mrs H— would have enjoyed the enthusiasm he shows here for joining in his teacher's stories. For Dean, reading stories is clearly a shared and pleasurable experience. It is interesting, too, that he singles out writing as the activity he enjoys most. Perhaps having learned already that reading has power to influence and to transmit enjoyment he can approach the productive side of language with confidence and a sense that writing is a way of organizing thoughts and feelings, not merely a series of plain, difficult hurdles for isolated and repeated practice.

> 3 *Miranda* (9): I like reading actually / I like to choose my own books / well Miss recommends them but she doesn't / um / force you to have them / she recommended the Lloyd Alexander books *Taran Wanderer* / then there's *The High King* / then there's *The Black Cauldron* and *The Castle of Llyr* / they're not really in that order because *The Black Cauldron* is first / and Miss has read them all and two of them were her own books / she asks you questions about the books / I've read a lot of Alan Garner's books and nearly all of Helen / Creswell's and the C. S. Lewis books / and *The Hobbit* is my favourite and the Lloyd Alexander books and I like / the / *Famous Five* books and the *Secret Seven* / sometimes I read a book a day and sometimes I read half of it /

There are several points here worth notice apart from Miranda's articulate way of talking about her reading. She can, of course, handle the term 'recommend'; but more than that, she is actually engaged in the business of recommendations where, as a reader, she is guided – not coerced or instructed – by her teacher. We notice Miranda's enthusiasm for reading revealed in both the *amount* she reads and in the *diversity* of what she enjoys. Such enthusiasm is part of the developing confidence a young reader requires to tackle new and challenging or complex material with the knowledge that reading can repay the effort with pleasure, satisfaction and information. Part of this process is the way her teacher has organized the chance for her pupils to talk over their reading so that, far from being a solitary, isolated pastime, story becomes an experience to be shared and linked to other classroom activities. Finally, though perhaps most important in establishing reading and story telling as natural activities, it is obvious that this pupil also perceives her teacher as a reader – one who is prepared to buy her own books and to share them with her pupils. No amount of exhortation can influence pupils' motivation to read as much as natural demonstrations that reading is something that adults normally do for pleasure and profit.

> 4 *Alison* (8):   Well we don't get much time for it really / we have our reading books you see and we have to read them if we have finished / our work / or if he goes out and then we can carry on and then he comes and says / put away your reading books and I keep reading the same bits over /

From what Alison says it appears that reading for her is in danger of becoming a peripheral activity – something which is only done to fill in time or when more important things cannot be done. It later transpired that she had not changed her 'reading book' since the end of the previous term and was less than half way through it: since she is not allowed to take her book home and since she has been taught not to value this kind of reading highly this is not surprising. She is clearly well on her way to the situation described by Lunzer and Gardner (1979) where reading is used primarily in secondary schools as a means of control. We can guess which of these four children are most likely to slip into Whitehead's 36 per cent of non-readers by the time they are 14. Whether children are compelled to read by browbeating (like Michael) or authority (like Alison) makes little difference. Unless they also develop for themselves the sense of pleasure and fulfilment that reading can offer, we cannot say that they experience reading as anything but superficial. It may be that adult pressure turns some children away from voluntary reading, as Maddock (1969) argued: 'there are those who resist reading because reading is something adults make them do' (p.90). The teacher must find ways of showing that reading has meaning, relevance and pleasure.

Discovering pupils' attitudes to reading should be part of this process, if only as one way of obtaining some feedback on whether teaching objectives have been reached or not. Bardgett (1977) agrees that if we make no attempt to probe a pupil's attitudes to reading and to take these into account in planning future learning, we are likely to generate reluctance rather than minimize it through 'our reluctance to understand . . . [the pupil's] way of life' (p.8).

The reading diet

Let us turn now to the second area of concern: the materials which children are encouraged to read or which perhaps they are denied access to. Consider this three-page extract from a popular reading scheme.

> 1 Come on, Pat.
> 2 Come and play in the boat, Jane.
> 3 Come on, he says.
> 4 Look at me in the boat.

5 Look at me, Jane.
6 Look at me, says Peter.
7 Get in the boat, Jane.
8 The fish can see you in the water.
9 Get in the boat, says Peter.
10 Peter can see a fish in the water.
11 They want to fish.
12 Jane is in the water and Peter is in the boat.
13 Jump up. Jump up here.
14 Come and play on the boat.
15 Come on the boat.
16 Come on, says Peter.
17 They like to play on the boat.
18 Jane and Peter play in the water.

We immediately recognize the style of a reading primer, with its short sentences, simple vocabulary, repetition of sounds, words and ideas, the standard characters (girl, boy and dog), the engagement in exciting activity at an interesting location (the seaside). It may well be difficult to move away from the staple elements that make up this familiar recipe. Such time-worn methods have apparently worked for many thousands of children and have been used successfully to nurture a (restricted) range of reading abilities. What we are talking about here are the problems that arise if a child's intellectual diet is confined to one staple input over a longish period of time. (Alison, we remember, had kept to the same book for several months.) Reading rickets is never easy to diagnose in its early stages!

Let us now take another look at how our reading primer material relates to what a child has already learned about language and meaning. Halliday (1969) has shown how very young children intuitively recognize the power of language to achieve a wide range of functions and satisfy many needs. To take just one example (what Halliday calls the heuristic model), the child soon discovers the power of questions as a way of learning. Young children of 2 or 3 will frequently practise this technique by asking strings of questions; they are very soon able to use questions to gain information and to make sense of their world.

Child: What are you putting those / biscuit things / on the wall for?
Adult: These are tiles / they're hard / look / feel one.
Child: Mm / how do they stick?
Adult: Can you see this cem / this sticky stuff here on the wall / then I stick /the tiles to it.
Child: Why are you putting the wavy lines on it?
Adult: So it sticks better.
Child: Why does it?

In exchanges with adults who try to correct their language structure, children attend exclusively to meaning. This is not surprising, since all their experience of language acquisition has shown them that language is a powerful tool for shaping and carving the meanings we exchange. A sometimes quoted typical example is the following:

Child: My teacher holded the baby rabbits and we patted them.
Adult: Did you say she held them tightly?
Child: No, she holded them loosely.

The child, as Halliday argues, learns about the immense and varied power of language intuitively and adults may try to impose an etiquette of correct grammatical structure too early when the child's natural focus is upon the content and meaning of communication. Frequently she/he does not even notice the restrictions adults place upon communication. It is as if the child also intuitively knows that the business of arranging words neatly on their correct hangers is best learned after mastering the art of dressing and undressing.

Now if we look again at the 18 numbered stages from the reading primer we can ask what it is that the child internalizes from the content. What meanings can be constructed from the cohesion and coherence of this episode? The scene is fairly clear. Peter (the boy) is engaged in activity and the passage, as well as narrating what happens, contains frequent exhortations to Jane (the girl) and to Pat (the dog), who are somewhat more passive, to get into the action. There are frequent exhortations to 'look' to 'come' to 'jump up' and to 'get in' both before and after the explicit and descriptive stage (12):

Jane is in the water and Peter is in the boat.

The causal links seem to be straightforward. Peter wants Jane to play with him in the boat (2) *because* they like to play on the boat (17). Within this framework other causal connections may be perceived, for example between 7 and 8: Jane is invited to get in the boat *because* the fish can see her while she remains out of it. This kind of connection seems reasonable since 11 tells us 'they want to fish'. (Presumably they will have more chance of catching a fish if it cannot see them.)

We have begun – as a child would need to – to make sense of a passage such as this. We have focused upon the setting in which the characters are placed and we have begun to make connections between the various stages of the events and episodes. However, as Macbeth once said when he was analysing the causal connections of a projected episode, 'We will proceed no further in this business.' Our sequence of numbered story stages 1–18, I must now reveal, is not as it appears in the original text. The elements do, in fact, come in order, *but the order is exactly reversed in the original book.*

Having reread the passage in its proper order, starting at 18 and finishing at 1, a reader will have established a similarly coherent picture to the one we have already discussed. This passage makes nearly as much sense when read back to front as when read in the intended order. We could speculate whether other arrangements of the 18 elements, even a random ordering, would make as much sense. Is such arbitrariness helpful to children who have reached the third book in their scheme? I would argue that at this time it is preferable, even essential, to use material where links, connections and relationships reinforce the patterns that a child has already learned exist in language and communication. It seems that some children have difficulty simply because the language of such readers appears arbitrary.

If emphasis is placed exclusively on either word recognition or on phonic teaching, repetitive practice may be vital. In fact, though, if there is no cohesive, forward-moving narrative the young reader is denied the cumulative help that logically ordered meanings give and may feel that there is little meaning in such 'texts'. We do not wish learners to shy away from reading, talking, writing and listening because language appears to them too unpredictable to order.

A second difficulty with materials of this kind is that of discovering the meaning they have in relation to the experiences of the reader. If readers do not recognize the verbal patterns they have already heard in real speech and in story, the text of reading primers is likely to be categorized as 'something different' by readers who will also have the difficulty of constructing a frame of reference for this new experience. If readers perceive no point of contact between the events and relationships in the reading matter and those in their own lives, they are in danger of rejecting the reading as pointless, isolated and disconnected from the world as they know it.

Whichever way we choose to read the three pages containing our 18 utterances – whether forwards, backwards or random – we notice the insistence of one protagonist that another gets into the boat. Utterances 1, 2, 3, 7, 9, 13, 14, 15 and 16 have this specific function. Rarely can so much exhortation have been used by one person in so short a space where the end result seems to matter so little. After a statement and the 8 repetitions which makes up 50 per cent of the sequence we move without warning to:

I want a cake please, says Peter.

The reader may be baffled by the connection between this and what has gone before. An illustration showing Jane preparing to climb into the boat only reinforces the lack of continuity. In the real world a boy who insists on someone doing something so stridently and repetitively surely cares about the result, which will crucially affect what happens next as well as his relationship with the other. In this case the incident, unresolved, is dropped. Adult and child readers can only draw their own conclusions. *Either* Peter's frenetic attempts to get Jane on the boat (for purposes known only to him) have exhausted and hungered him beyond bearing or we are in a literary world where motivation, cause and effect, relationships and behaviour are unrelated to experience, whether actual or imagined.

It is not my intention here to criticize one particular reading scheme. I want instead to draw attention to the potential conflict caused in the minds of children by any reading which promotes arbitrariness instead of pattern, disconnection rather than coherence and emptiness rather than fulfilment. Even a casual look at other reading schemes will produce examples rather worse than the one we have taken. Again it is necessary to add that if children are also exposed to a wide range of 'real' books little harm will come to them; if their diet is restricted to reading primers then some cases of reading rickets will surely follow.

A child presented with

This is Dan.
Dan has a cat.
The cat is Pat.
Can you see Pat?
Pat is in the bag.
Pat is a fat cat.

may not perceive that someone somewhere with a penchant for phonics has decided that at this particular stage in reading the learner requires practice in decoding words containing the short 'a' sound. But the child will have no difficulty in associating this kind of vocabulary and structure with 'reading' books and 'teaching reading'. There is the apocryphal story of the witness to a road accident who ran along the street to find a policeman.

'Come, come. Come and look', she cried agitatedly.
'Hang on a minute', said the policeman, and speaking into his walkie-talkie began, 'A teacher has just reported an accident.'

The difference between reading-primer kind of language and the language of story is that the latter essentially communicates meaning – which is why the child has bothered to internalize language. We should always ask what *meanings* are being communicated by the reading materials that we introduce children to. Of course, it is possible that all 5 year olds have noticed that men frequently carry cats around in bags when they get too fat to walk around for themselves! On the other hand, such unconnected snippets may make reading harder for children who cannot recognize in them the connections and coherence they have noticed in the real world.

Tinkering about with bits of language divorced from reality and usage may give a child strange notions about what language is and what it is for. Classes of children are still urged to 'Give the feminine of *bullock* and *marquis*' or to 'Write two separate sentences each containing the word *obelisk*'. It is just conceivable that a child may find some use for this dislocated word play – though only just! The fatuity of most of this kind of linguistic dabbling is illustrated by one 10 year old who was engaged in an exercise where she was faced with providing opposites of random words in a list. She had come to the word 'malevolent'. Looking over her shoulder the visitor to her classroom saw that she had confidently written her answer: 'femalevolent'. It is always worth asking just what they are learning.

A further, more extensive, example will show the difference between the use of isolated and coherent uses of language in the classroom. A girl in the 7–8 age group was engaged on two separate occasions with two different exercises from textbooks. To the first request, 'Write a sentence about each of the pictures', she produced the following:

1 My first picture has a kitten on it.
2 There is a duck on the next one.
3 This is a picture of me.
4 In the picture you can see a picture of a ship.

To the second request, 'Use *so* to join the two parts of the sentences', she produced:

My puppy was hungry so I gave it some food.
I had twenty pence so I bought a rubber ball.
The baby was asleep so we spoke softly.

On the face of it these seem to place an emphasis on sequence, order and logic. But this sequence is superficial. We can imagine connections between a kitten, a duck, a person and a ship or between a puppy, a rubber ball and a baby. Clearly, though, this is not the point of these exercises where meaning certainly stops at the limits of each sentence. The purpose is elsewhere: perhaps to discover if this girl can construct and join sentences and use the conventions of full stop and capital letter. In these respects it also looks as if this learner was successful and, to the important question we posed previously, the response might be that she is learning construction, joining and the conventions of written language.

The problem with this kind of judgement is that it is made in just as much isolation as her exercises are set. Judgements about learning need to be made in the context of the child, her abilities and needs. When we examine her use of language on previous occasions we find in a book she is reading and enjoying passages like this:

There on a throne hung with crimson silk sat his grandfather watching. Perseus bent down and picked up the last quoit. With all his might he threw it, while the crowd cheered. Then without warning, a gust of wind blew in from the sea, caught the quoit and blew it straight towards the throne where the King was sitting.

A piece of writing she did on a previous occasion provides this example:

One day I found myself in Topsy Turvey Lane and people wear hats on their feet. So I walked down the streets where boats go on the streets and then a very strong old man came up to me and said good bye, he said don't come to my house so I presume he meant come to my house. So I followed him and when I got there his dog was wearing Wellington boots.

It is immediately obvious that in both writing and reading the learner is here using language in which sequence and logical order operate. Moreover, they operate not merely at sentence level, but over extended discourse. The continuous writing, as well as revealing her ability to construct and join sentences and to practise the conventions of written English, also provides the opportunity to draw upon stories previously read and to construct a similar one. It displays a developing ability to take account of and to interest her audience. The extract more specifically reveals the writer's ability to use the word 'so' to link ideas and units of language.

This last point forces us to ask again what the point was of asking her to do the joining exercise with the word 'so'. Where is the relevance and the need to extend her ability in teaching her something she can already do? When looked at in the context of what this girl knows and can do naturally the emptiness of the exercise is apparent. It is as though a child who has already designed and made a chest of drawers and studied plans for making a record cabinet were condemned to produce only practice dovetail joints. When we ask exactly what children are learning we must ask whether we are teaching what they already know. The consequences of failing to interest and extend learners will be seen in their future attitude and response to teaching. The isolated exercises we have looked at do not provide half the learning opportunities (or satisfaction) that engaging with narrative in reading or writing can do. Neither do they achieve their specific objectives as well as shaping or recreating narrative can.

Reading, like other uses of language, operates in a context, and decontextualized exercises, whether in phonic or look-and-say form, are likely to have unfortunate effects on large numbers of children who, resisting the aridity of content and fearing failure, never become willing readers. As the Cox Committee (DES 1988a) wisely say, 'Teachers should recognise that reading is a complex but unitary process and not a set of discrete skills which can be taught separately in turn and, ultimately, bolted together' (9.7). Apart from emphasizing the unitary process of reading itself, the links between experience and reading and between reading and other modes of language use are crucial. For example, young readers are able to use their experience of reality to inform their guesses about the meaning of written texts. Similarly, knowledge of written forms of language, based, say, on the stories they have had read to them, can be used to help anticipate the order in which words come in reading. Faced with 'Jim lived in a little—with four rooms', the reader can *predict* (from meaning) that the word must be a place to live in like 'house', 'flat' or 'cottage' and (from syntax) that the word is likely to be a noun or another adjective. The remainder of the sentence *confirms* these judgements and rules out the possibility of the adjective. So the reader uses anticipation and evidence derived from a knowledge of language and the world where language is used to make these active reconstructions of the text. In this way reading becomes a process of reducing uncertainty (Smith 1971). In contrast, a young reader who has been taught word recognition and phonic skills in isolation from meaning may have difficulty with a word like 'house', where the word shape and sound are not vastly different from, say, 'horse'. This is not to argue that phonic and look-and-say methods are inappropriate; rather that they serve the reader best incidentally, when the emphasis is on the interpretations of *meaning* and not merely on the decoding of print. It does mean, however, that the abilities to predict, to anticipate, to check and to confirm and to make judgements should be developed as basic skills and not left until the latter stages of some artificial reading taxonomy of objectives, as 'higher-order' skills.

It follows that reading schemes which do not assist in the 'reduction of uncertainty' will cause difficulty for some learners and that those which emphasize visual and auditory skills in isolation from meaning may make reading unnecessarily complex and uninviting.

A reading scheme, because of its serial construction, often beginning with small skills and leading to more complex ones (from little words to big ones and longer sentences), suggests there is a single set of stepping stones from confusion to clarity. The numbered series of books represent the safely sequenced stages in a journey across the swirling muddy depths of reading practice. Why is it, then, that so many children founder or enter the water with extreme reluctance? The truth is that there are as many ways to cross a stream as there are to skin a cat. An important way for many learners will be to build their own bridges from their own knowledge of language and of reading as a pleasure-giving pursuit. For others, the context in which their progress in reading is measured will unfortunately be constrained by as many pitfalls and moral strictures as that other Pilgrim who was finally taken into the promised land.

With reading, we cannot afford to be selective in our intake. Success in reading is necessary to every child. Its pleasure is every child's right and literacy is a prerequisite for every fully participating member of a modern society.

The sustenance of story

Now let us examine one or two stories for children to ascertain in what respects they contain extra sustenance and relate to reality. If we take John Burningham's (1974) illustrated story *The Snow* as an example, we find a sentence structure similar to the one we looked at earlier.

1 One day it snowed.
2 Mummy and I rolled a big snowball.
3 We made a snowman.
4 I sat on the sledge.
5 Mummy pulled me.
6 But I fell off.
7 I lost my glove and I was cold.
8 So we went indoors.
9 I hope the snow is here tomorrow.

Even if the ingredients look the same, it is immediately obvious that little sense could be made out of these 9 elements by reading them in reverse: the story progresses forwards only. It can be categorized according to systems of story analysis and grammar (see Stein and Glenn 1979) and it therefore fits into the child's perception of what a story is. The logical connections are clear to a young reader who has rolled a snowball *then* used it to make a snowman and who has gone indoors for warmth *after* falling into snow. The same young reader has opportunity to extract considerable meaning from the story. The last line (9) links with other reflections about experience that the child may have engaged in. The child in the story looks forward to other experiences in the magical, exciting snow despite having experienced discomfort. The child reader is allowed to contemplate this desire and to reflect how like (or unlike) the fictional child's his/her own feelings are.

Another splendid story with pictures and text is *Rosie's Walk* by Pat Hutchins. The elements of this story may appear random but they are logically ordered as parts of one coherent sentence.

Rosie the hen
went for a walk
across the yard
around the pond
over the haycock,
past the mill,
through the fence,
under the beehives,
and got back in time for dinner.

I do not propose to analyse the meaning of this story in detail since it has already been done by Margaret Spencer (1976) in a valuable article called 'Stories are for telling'. (The reader is strongly recommended to read this.) Margaret Spencer notes in this story the nature of anticipation and climax and the way the reader's expectations are modified, as in 'real stories'. But the whole point and pleasure of the story is contained in the relationship between the text and the illustrations which show Rosie pursuing her promenade unconcernedly and oblivious of the fox pursuing her! That fox has nasty accidents in the yard, the pond, the haycock, the mill and finally with the beehives and, as Margaret Spencer says, 'the reader, himself a story-teller, *makes it mean*' (her italics, p.21). This is an important point for, in the best stories, the story teller leaves room for an audience or reader to supply meaning to the story. It is the reader who makes the connection between the text and the fox's actions and so provides the pleasure of contemplating the irony of a villain 'hoist with his own petard' who gets his come-uppance.

One further example of 'real stories' is *Whistle for Willie* by Ezra Jack Keats (1964). This story is too long to quote in its entirety but this is how it begins.

1 Oh, how Peter wished he could whistle!
2 He saw a boy playing with his dog. Whenever
   the boy whistled, the dog ran straight to him.
3 Peter tried and tried to whistle, but he
   couldn't. So instead he began to turn himself
   around – around and around he whirled . . .
   faster and faster . . .
4 When he stopped
   everything turned
   down . . .
   and up . . .
5 and up . . .
   and down . . .
   and around
   and around.

The forward movement of this narrative, with its logical connections and consequences, is immediately apparent; so is the way the writer has made repetition (evoking whirling and dizziness) necessary and functional instead of artificial and clumsy. Whenever Peter cannot whistle – the story is about his frequent practice and eventual success – he reverts to a familiar pastime such as chalking lines, spinning round, dressing up, walking lines, playing with his shadow. He has already perfected these occupations and they provide him with solace and amusement while he gathers himself for another attack on the important task. A child reader is invited to make this connection personally and can hardly avoid recognizing in Peter's situation a natural desire to become grown up. This is symbolized for Peter by the magnificent skill of whistling. Little else in a child's own experience presents the opportunity for contemplation in the complex and interwoven way that a powerful story can.

It is more than likely that the child reader or listener will profit from this kind of reflection, understanding of course, as in *The Snow*, that minor discomforts do not mean that the anticipation of future pleasure is reduced. After all, the child who scrapes a knee by falling from a bike one day is usually keen to ride it again the next – or even sooner.

I make no apology for analysing the meaning of children's stories, although I know objections are sometimes raised by those who wish everything presented to children to remain simple, uncluttered and undissected. I am not suggesting that children should participate in the analysis themselves. However, if an interested parent or teacher goes even further to make connections between stories like *The Snow* and adult stories like *Macbeth*, for example, then perhaps the essential point becomes clearer still. The adult watching Macbeth deliberating whether or not to kill Duncan has probably never been in exactly the same situation; but he or she can still make connections with personal experience and with occasions when a moral dilemma had to be resolved. The occasions in our experience where it seemed we could gain an advantage only at the expense of someone else can be related to Macbeth's situation. We thereby understand his 'vaulting ambition', empathize with and feel pity for him as he agonizes and obtain a new perspective on the moral choices we have to make ourselves.

It must not be supposed that this kind of argument is elitist or that the recommendation is that every child be forced to see *Macbeth* at the earliest possible age. The essential point is that some reading material has within it food for the mind and for the feelings and some reading material has neither. (*The Snow* and *Macbeth* are in this respect part of the same continuum.) It is the emotional and intellectual sustenance a child receives from reading stories that make the same child want to go on reading. I would criticize materials of the 'See Spot. Run Spot. Run.' variety not only because, as Halliday (1969) says, they bear little relation to the language as a child has learned to use it, but because they make of narrative something apart from life as it is lived and they turn the food of story into a dry biscuit.

Adults can intervene positively in children's reading; indeed they must do so.

Stories may need to be introduced, presented, recommended, talked over and savoured together. The links with experience must be fostered and reflection encouraged. We remember Miranda's teacher intervening successfully in this way. There is little point in leaving all children to find their own way through a bewildering menu.

Using story at school

It is, of course, easy to acknowledge the power of story and still teach in ways which contradict such awareness. Observations of nursery and primary class-rooms show that story is used by teachers in various ways; but these still permit generalization.

Story telling is usually a whole-group activity. It can be used as an incentive: 'If you behave, I'll read you a story'. It frequently occurs at the end of a school session where the aim may be to relax and control the group or where 'pressure' is taken off and the child is permitted to enjoy a pleasurable experience presented by the teacher. Studies of talk in nursery and infant schools have shown that much time is spent on the organizational and administrative aspects of dealing with pupils and in the 'here and now'.

The authors of one study (Wood *et al*. 1980) examined the talk of teachers with their pre-school pupils and summarized as follows (pp.100–1):

> At best, then, only one quarter of the time spent in talk was given over to considering the way people and things tick, to telling stories about events in the past or looking forward to things that might happen.

Of course it is possible that even when story is used, the way of presenting it may limit the learning. It is perfectly possible even with young children to use story purely as a kind of oral comprehension exercise with the teacher pausing every now and again to demand recall on some point of fact from the child audience.

Teacher: What did the crocodile do? John.
John: He / er / he bit the monkey.
Teacher: No he didn't / did he? / you weren't listening John.

Whenever strategies become routinized in this way, learning opportunities shrink. It is also likely that if story is used primarily as testing material for recall then pupils are likely to learn that what the teacher wants is for information to be remembered and reproduced. If the testing of children's recall publicly is stressful, then this is likely to interfere with enjoyment and so undermine the teacher's main aim. The same process of contraction may also occur in the stories which children tell themselves. These are frequently organized into a 'news' period where children are encouraged to tell stories about their own experiences and events in their own lives. Traditionally such periods often come at the beginning of a week or day and the child is encouraged to tell a 'story' orally and then, when writing abilities have developed, in written form. This strategy can be used valuably as a way of offering responsibility and creative experience in formulating ideas in words and is also an important way of showing that the learner's own experiences are seen as valid and valuable by the school. On the other hand, routine and the child's ability to 'play the system' can reduce this activity to an empty, repetitive formula. Consider this piece of writing by Mark, a 10 year old, about the experience of 'news time' in his infant school.

> When I was in the Infants we used to have News every Monday morning and when we had finished talking about it we went off and wrote about it, and every Monday morning without fail I wrote, 'I played football with my brother', or 'I went to my Nans'. But one morning when I wrote 'I played football with my brother', my teacher said, 'I'm getting fed up with you writing the same things every morning. Go away and write something different for change.'
>
> 'Alright', I said. I went and wrote, 'I went to my Nans', and from then, I thought that I would write that every week when we had News.

There is not much point in following a routine unless we also consider ways of extending a pupil's learning, ways in which we can intervene effectively in the learning process and ways in which we can create opportunities for pupils to formulate *new* ideas and experiences. Mark, we suspect, has the ability to do just enough to keep out of trouble. But, of course, the problem of shrinking curricular opportunities is not confined to the infant school nor to able pupils. Since our focus is on story let us use an extract from a story to illustrate the problem which faces a 'less able' boy in a secondary school. Jan Mark's admirable book *Thunder and Lightnings* (1978) is about Victor, a boy who is not so good at things (like reading and writing) that his school values, but who is given the task of showing round a new boy, Andrew.

> 'Miss Beale said you would show me round, to look at the projects', said Andrew.
>
> 'Why, do you want to copy one?' asked Victor, lifting a strand of hair and exposing one eye. 'You could copy mine, only someone might recognise it. I've done that three times already.'
>
> 'Whatever for?' said Andrew, 'Don't you get tired of it?' Victor shook his head and his hair.
>
> 'That's only once a year. I did that two times at the junior school and now I'm doing that again', he said. 'I do fish, every time. Fish are easy. They're all the same shape.'
>
> 'No, they're not', said Andrew.
>
> 'They are when I do them', said Victor. He spun his book round, with one finger, to show Andrew the drawings. His fish were not only all the same shape, they were all the same shape as slugs. Underneath each drawing was a printed heading: BRAEM; TENSH; CARP; STIKLBACK; SHARK. It was the only way of telling them apart. The shark and the bream were identical, except that the shark had a row of teeth like tank traps.
>
> 'Isn't there a "c" in stickleback?' said Andrew.
>
> Victor looked at his work. 'You're right.' He crossed out both 'k's, substituted 'c's and pushed the book away, the better to study it. 'I got that wrong last year.'
>
> Andrew flipped over a few pages. There were more slugs: PLACE; COD; SAWFISH; and a stringy thing with a frill round its neck: EEL.

'Don't you have to write anything?' asked Andrew.

'Yes, look, I wrote a bit back here. About every four pages will do', said Victor. 'Miss Beale, she keep saying I ought to write more but she's glad when I don't. She's got to read it.'

'Project' can become as stereotyped as 'news' or 'story'. The remarkable thing is how amenably children will jump through the same hoops, practising skills already acquired, keeping to safe ground, unwilling to take risks and become tentative in the way that leads to learning.

In order to offer alternatives to the routinized approaches described, the next part is unashamedly practical. It offers suggestions for and strategies working with story based upon the argument in Chapters 1 and 2. It also presents an annotated and classified list of suitable materials for children aged 3–13.

PART TWO
Reading: the first two key stages

3 Organizing for reading 3–7

CHRIS BURMAN

English for Ages 5–11 (DES 1988a, 2.5) uses David Allen's words to describe how successful language teachers 'need to organise the learning in ways which follow on logically and consistently from the successful language learning which children have already accomplished in the context of their own homes and communities'. This chapter seeks to analyse the essential features of this context and to suggest ways in which the teacher can ensure continuity by translating some of the principles into supportable classroom practice. In doing so it accepts that children will have reached widely different stages of development depending on their prior experiences both within and outside the home. Some will not have been as 'fortunate' as those discussed in the report in that they may not have had as many opportunities to engage in meaningful literacy events and to develop understanding of the purposes and nature of written language (see 2.3). A 'developmental' view of language and literacy learning recognizes this diversity. In particular a 'real-book' or shared-reading approach offers opportunities for all children at all stages of development to meet with success.

In the past teachers have often tended to teach all children like the ones who have come from literate homes, when some have obviously not had the same chances as others. Kevin was such a child. His story illustrates what can all too often happen when 'inexperienced' readers are taught formal 'schooled literacy' and fail to make sense of its rules and abstractions. He also shows how an 'apprenticeship' or real-book approach can change the reading climate, the child's view of reading and of himself not only as a reader but as a learner.

Kevin's story

Kevin, a shy, sensitive boy, had not been given a reading book during his first year at school. He had great difficulty learning the reading scheme vocabulary and so his teacher gave him pre-reading, visual and auditory games and exercises, to try to develop 'reading readiness'. By the time he was 6 and in middle infants, he had still not moved on from the word-tin stage.

Not surprisingly, he had developed a negative self-image as a reader *and* as a learner, for all the months of reading drills and exercises had led to frustration and anxiety. School, for Kevin, was where he frequently met failure and where emphasis was placed on what he could *not* do rather than on what he could do. The school had given him a view of reading as a task that was difficult, meaningless and pointless. What counted as reading in the reception class was whether you could recognize isolated words out of context to command and, if you were lucky, to read pages in books that were then ticked on a card. The worst thing of all was that most children in the class were able to do those things and Kevin could not.

The nature of the difficulty

Kevin's family were not book orientated, they did not visit the library, read for pleasure or buy many books. Kevin had not been read stories and was, therefore, not one of the 'fortunate children' described in *English for Ages 5–11* (2.3). Kevin's parents were, however, loving and caring and appeared resigned to the fact that he was following a family pattern of late development and 'slow reading'.

Kevin had, therefore, come to school knowing very little about the nature and purposes of written language. His concepts of print were still undeveloped and in particular he had yet to understand that a word represented a single unit of meaning. Research has shown that many children, on entry to school, are 'inexperienced' in this way (Reid 1966; Downing 1974, 1985). Donaldson (1978, p.97) points out that many children have problems learning to read because they do not realize that the flow of speech can be broken into separate words.

> This realisation is indispensable if they are to deal sensibly with the grouped and spaced marks on paper, which as they must now come to see, correspond with the spoken language.

Downing (1985) sees the difficulty to be one of a lack of 'cognitive clarity' or the lack of 'clear understanding of the features and functions of concepts of literacy' (p.43). In other words, for children like Kevin at this stage in conceptual development, 'the penny hasn't dropped'.

In school, the rote learning of words, when he had not formed the underlying concept, led to further cognitive confusion rather than understanding. Try as he could, Kevin was unable to make sense of all the fragmented bits and pieces of language presented in exercises, word-tins and flash cards. The teaching had in fact got in the way of learning.

The way forward

Kevin needed to develop a collaborative partnership with an adult who would mediate, read *with* him and help him make sense of reading. Frank Smith (1978a) has said that the beginning reader has one overriding need: for learning to read to make sense, and *English for Ages 5–11* affirms that (9.4).

Reading is much more than the decoding of black marks upon a page: it is a quest for meaning and one which requires the reader to be an active participant. It is a pre-requisite of successful teaching of reading especially in the early stages that whenever techniques are taught or books are chosen for children's use, meaning should always be in the foreground.

Kevin was allowed to choose from a selection of picture books, which included books by Pat Hutchins, Ron Maris, John Burningham and David McKee. Such authors and their texts can initiate the beginning reader into understanding the vital rules of the game, such as how to interpret pictures, how to anticipate and predict likely words and phrases, how to use the context and structure of the sentence and unravel meaning. Psycholinguistic theories about the nature of the reading process now focus more attention on the use of such clueing systems and much less on word and letter identification (Smith 1978a). Margaret Clark (1976) states that (p.4):

> It is important to define the task of reading as predicting one's way through print and to focus even in the beginning of teaching reading on anticipation and prediction rather than identification.

At another level, quality picture books provoke a powerful and emotional response in young children. John Burningham's stories, for instance, have instant appeal, dealing with dogs in the garden, lost rabbits, messy babies and friends who sometimes fall out! Through such themes children come to recognize their own culture, needs, feelings and interests. They promote positive feelings about stories, characters and make learning to read easier because what the child *feels* about reading ultimately affects how easy or difficult she/he finds the task. Kevin, as we have seen, had an urgent need for learning to read to be made easier and for all the effort and energy to be made worthwhile.

The approach used to help Kevin is described in full in Liz Waterland's *Read With Me: An Apprenticeship Approach to Reading* (1985). The main features of this approach are:

- The child chooses the book.
- The adult and child read together, the child taking over the reading at easy parts.
- The focus of attention is shared enjoyment and meaning.
- The adult can finger point to direct attention to the print.
- The child can be encouraged to 'guess' and 'have a go' at reading parts of the text independently, especially if it is highly predictable.
- The child may try to read the text later for him or herself using various clues like pictures, rhyme, general sense and the structure of language.

Although early independent reading may not be entirely accurate, frequent rereading allows the pupil to gradually match the 'story in the head' to the appropriate words on the page (see Chapter 3, 'The role of the child: taking a closer look').

Towards success

After only a few weeks of shared reading Kevin began to lose his fear of failure, grew in confidence and found that reading had a great deal to offer. Time and time again he would say, 'I can read this!'; 'I can do it!'; 'This one's easy for me!' He wanted to be a reader, to behave like a reader and he believed he was a reader.

He was able to take control of his own reading and of his own progress, in a way which provoked a new sense of his own power and status. He would often interrupt a story to interpret some of the hidden messages in the pictures and elucidate meanings. In *My Book* by Ron Maris he explained with laughter, 'look see the book wot da boy's reading, I'm reading it to you!'

He was intrigued and excited by the books: they seemed to draw him into the stories, engage his feelings and explore themes which spoke to him in a special way. This stimulated a great deal of talk. The striking feature of this talk was the urgency to draw on real-life experience and relate the text to himself and himself to the text. We can see Kevin doing this after reading John Burningham's *The Dog*:

> 'We don't have no creatures, my brother's bird died. It died on his birthday, that's why he was so sad on his birthday.'

The kind of talk that went on around the stories developed Kevin's abilities to think beyond the here and now and enabled him to detach his thinking and reflect on experience. After reading *Titch* (Pat Hutchins), he said:

> 'I bet she wishes she didn't give Titch the seed now.'

Wells (1981) describes this self-conscious and reflective attitude to experience as the mark of true literacy in that it encourages the development of higher level cognitive skills. He claims that unless children are encouraged to acquire literacy as a tool for, and a spur to, higher levels of thinking, then learning will be adversely affected.

In this way Kevin's view of reading changed dramatically as he came to see reading as an active, creative, problem-solving activity. After two terms of shared reading in school and at home he had developed a much stronger understanding of written language and its forms and functions. *The Dog* (J. Burningham) was his favourite because, 'I can look at the words in this 'cos it's easy to look at the words in this one'. He was able to tackle unfamiliar texts by using sight words learnt in context and by using various strategies: the use of the general sense; the patterns of language and sentence structure; initial letter sound clues, etc. Like an 'experienced' reader, he now knew the need to keep going and predict his way through unfamiliar texts.

The teacher's role had been crucial in helping to create a different kind of climate for reading and a different view of the reading task. She had given support and encouragement for risk taking and endless reassurance to help him face what he feared. With her guidance he had discovered what reading was all about.

This kind of collaborative partnership in reading and learning is the model used by the successful parent in the literate home. It is one in which parents intuitively initiate children into the literacy-learning process before they start school. We can see the similarities as it is represented in the model in Figure 3.1. Gordon Wells' study of children learning language at home (Wells 1987) has cast new light on the role of parents in early language development. He writes (p.194):

> There are many ways in which parents foster their child's development in these years, not least through the quality of their conversation with them. But what this study clearly demonstrates is that it is growing up in a literate family environment, in which reading and writing are naturally occurring daily activities, that gives children a particular advantage when they start their formal education.

RESPONDS TO THE CHILD'S NEEDS AND INTERESTS
- Follows child's lead – lets child choose topic/time
- Focuses on meaning – sustains and develops interest through conversation
- Builds knowledge and understanding

USES LITERACY AND HIGHLIGHTS ITS VALUE AND PURPOSE
- Environmental print – signs/adverts
- Informational print – phone books/recipes etc
- Recreational print – fiction/non-fiction

SHARES THE SPECIAL PLEASURES OF WRITTEN LANGUAGE
Reads stories to and with child and helps child to:
- Make meaning
- Expand knowledge of books and narrative form
- Understand differences between spoken language and language of books
- Express ideas and feelings
- Think
- Develop linguistic resources
- Learn about self and the world
- See reading as a sociable, rewarding, shared, natural activity

---

FACILITATES
- Expects child to learn
- Allows experimentation
- Expects/allows mistakes
- Provides security
- Gives time
- Uses family shared experiences to facilitate learning and understanding

---

TEACHES – INCIDENTALLY AND INTUITIVELY
- Supports
- Encourages
- Guides
- Makes learning easy

Figure 3.1   Successful language learning at home: the role of the parent

WHAT DOES THE CHILD DO?

- Shows curiosity about written language
- Tries to make sense of it/puzzles things out
- Guesses at the functions of print, at what the message might be, why print is there and what it might say
- Makes mistakes and learns from them
- Uses language for own purposes
- Has control and ownership of own use of language and over own reading, writing, speaking, listening and thinking
- Develops a sense of power over language
- Is personally motivated to engage in reading and writing activities
- Chooses topics, Chooses time – engages in spontaneous language activities
- Programmes self – own level – own pace
- Tries things out, takes risks
- Learns while using language (the focus being not on the skills but the meaning)
- ACTS AS A PROBLEM SOLVER

Figure 3.2   Language learning at home: the role of the child

Kevin's teacher was able to re-create a similarly *favourable enabling literacy-learning climate* where written language was used to give pleasure and information and to provide security and personal satisfaction. Learning in school was made as easy as learning at home because the focus was on real purpose, meaning and pleasure. The teacher was also able to redefine Kevin's needs as a learner and allow him to take on the normal pattern of language learning. Some of its essential features are described in Figure 3.2.

To summarize at this point, we have seen how children need an enabling, supportive literacy-learning climate if they are to develop true insight and understanding. When they start school, however, children will have reached widely different stages of literacy development, depending on their experiences at home and their opportunities for understanding the nature and purposes of print in daily life. The teacher's task must, therefore, be to provide a developmental programme which recognizes this diversity and the need to cater for all children's needs within this continuum. An approach to reading which uses 'real' books and an 'apprenticeship' model is able to meet such a challenge and offer opportunities, for all children, at all stages of development and from all different backgrounds, to meet with success.

What follows are practical guidelines on how to transfer some of the essential principles and features of successful language teaching and learning into supportable classroom practice.

1 *The context*
   The kind of classroom environment which will 'enable' and foster language and literacy development.

2 *The role of the teacher*
   How knowledge gained from an understanding of the enabling parent can be
   used to help pupils acquire and develop literacy at school.
3 *The role of the child*
   How learning can continue to be active, meaningful and creative in the
   classroom situation.

The context for learning: the classroom environment

The book corner

This can be a general assembly area where children can choose books at various
times of the day. Here they can browse, develop preferences, learn to care for
books and develop the positive attitude that books matter. Children should have
time to share books; to enjoy private reading or simply to watch others and in so
doing to learn how to be a reader. The book corner can be the focal point for
shared meaning and enjoyment as a whole class and where reading is seen as a
sociable, rewarding, shared activity.

Criteria for the selection of books
Books should have text that is as near as possible to normal speech, with sentence
structures that are simple and easy to sort out; these natural language patterns act

Figure 3.3   Time for practice – to enjoy private or shared-reading sessions

as clues that guide towards meaning. Texts which have a strong rhythm and pattern when read aloud can carry a child through a book's difficulties, encouraging anticipation and prediction but also giving a sense of security similar to that provided by a nursery rhyme or skipping song, e.g. *Brown Bear, Brown Bear, What Do You See?* (Bill Martin Jnr); *Better Move on Frog* (Ron Maris); *The Elephant and the Bad Baby* (Raymond Briggs). Wordless books like Jan Ormerod's *Moonlight* and Pat Hutchins' *Changes, Changes* also encourage children to 'read' the 'text' and process each visual image and link it to the next; with practice they learn how to predict each new episode in the story.

Books should be selected carefully for good quality illustrations that act as powerful cues towards meaning and are an essential part of the story. Beginning readers need to learn to interpret pictures and use the information to build up a total impression of what is going on. They have to be able to move, to and fro, from text to pictures to match what they read with what they see. Picture books, therefore, need to integrate text and pictures so that the meaning of the words is deepened by the pictures and the feeling of the pictures is strengthened by the words (Waterland 1985).

The book corner includes nursery rhyme books; poetry anthologies; song books; non-fiction; children's cookery books; dual-language texts; catalogues; children's encyclopaedias; dictionaries; newspapers; comics, etc. Providing a wide range of print in a variety of written materials enriches the literacy environment and offers opportunities for pupils to experience many different language forms.

Figure 3.4   A listening centre

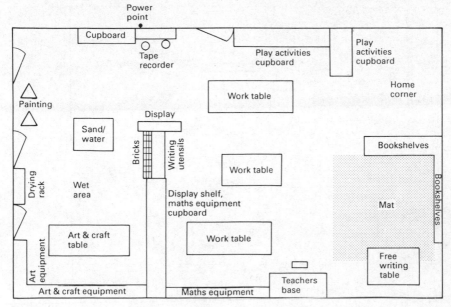

Class 6 Stirchley (RECEPTION)   Miss Wain

Figure 3.5   Organizing a reception class

A listening centre

Reading stories aloud is an essential part of a shared reading, 'real'-book programme. The listening area provides opportunities for children to hear stories read with expression, either through published tapes accompanying story-based programmes like *Story Chest* (Arnold Wheaton) or through teacher-made tapes of favourite picture books. For bilingual pupils, taped stories can be made available in their mother tongue (see *Stories for the Multi-lingual Primary Classroom*, ILEA 1983).

A reception classroom

Figure 3.5 is one way of organizing a classroom for the various activities which include listening, writing, reading and group talk. An alternative way of organizing a similar space follows, together with descriptions of the story castle, displays, writing and role-playing areas.

In this school three classrooms have been converted into three areas for science, maths and language. Figure 3.6 shows a plan of the language area. The labels on displays are all written in different community languages as well as English. A quiet book corner has been created using rolls of corrugated card, cut to the shape of a castle. The little girl in the illustration (Figure 3.7) is in the 'story castle' reading a book to her doll.

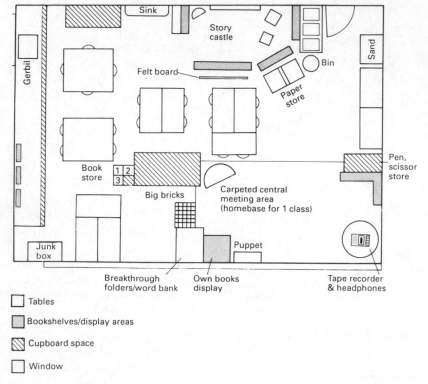

Figure 3.6   A language area
Reproduced by kind permission from Carol Brammer

The writing area

This can be resourced with different coloured and sized paper; different writing implements; glue; sugar-paper and sellotape, etc. so that children can behave as writers and acquire the habits of 'having a go' and of trying things out for themselves. They can 'write' messages to Mum, friends, teachers, make little greetings cards or draw/write about personal events and experiences. Bilingual pupils can write in their preferred language.

Role-play areas

Writing paper and implements, note pads and scrap paper can be included in play areas so that children can 'play' at reading and writing, imitate adult literacy events, reinforce understanding and see the exploration of print as rewarding. A home corner can be transformed into a class cafe where children can write a 'menu' for the day, take orders for meals and create decorative or informative signs and displays (see *English for Ages 5–11*, pp.51–2).

Organizing the physical environment for language learning in this way offers

Figure 3.7   The story castle

opportunities for pupils to take on the whole act first, however imperfectly and approximately and refine the parts later through experience and practice. But adults need to focus and furnish these experiences and act as models and supporters if they are to promote reading growth and understanding. It is this role which we now focus upon in our second dimension.

The role of the teacher

We saw earlier how important the reading aloud of stories was in developing young pre-school children's understanding of the value and purpose of written language. Reading and telling stories aloud has always been a feature of infant education but recent research (e.g. Wade 1984) has shed new light on the process and its crucial role in early literacy development. What it seems to do is help children overcome the considerable difficulties presented by the abstract nature of print. When adults read aloud with expression and gesture, they make the print 'come alive' and aid the comprehension of unusual language structures that are quite different from the kinds of language used in practical contexts and around everyday happenings.

But reading aloud performs many other functions (Figure 3.8). Gordon Wells' research in Bristol has focused even more attention on this process. He found that 'of all the activities that were characteristic of literate homes, it was the sharing of stories that was found to be most important' (see *Meaning Makers* 1987, p.194).

WHY READ STORIES ALOUD?
- It excites children's interest in reading
- It attracts them to wanting to learn to read
- It increases familiarity with the language of books and stories and with the patterns and rhythms of the written word
- It encourages reading with expression
- It develops understanding that reading is about making meaning
- It develops understanding of how books work
  where they begin and end
  how to turn over the pages
  how to read from left to right
  how to enjoy the pictures
- It encourages talking and thinking
- It develops important reading skills and strategies
- It promotes reading as a shared, natural, social activity

Figure 3.8   The functions of reading aloud

Using enlarged texts: The Hungry Giant (Story Chest, *Arnold Wheaton*)

First of all the class looks at the pictures on the front cover and the teacher encourages interpretation by asking questions like: 'What kind of giant do you think he is? Why do you think he is so cross? What do you think he will do? What will happen in the story?' This encourages anticipation and prediction, reading strategies now recognized as vital for success in becoming a 'real' reader. Smith (1978a,b), Goodman (1973a and 1973b) and others in the field of psycholinguistics have questioned the effectiveness of word-identification and decoding drills and exercises, especially in the early stages. Word by word accuracy is now considered far less important than making sense and the most efficient way to make sense, it is now believed, is to anticipate and predict a way through the text.

The story can then be read to the whole class, with the teacher pointing to the words as she reads, stopping when and where appropriate to discuss events, characters or pictures. Plenty of time should be allowed for talk, for children to put ideas into words, to share and explore their feelings and to think. They can be asked to guess: 'What will happen next? Where will the people go to find honey? What will the giant do next?' This builds confidence and encourages the use of the sense of the story. The most successful readers are often the ones who are most proficient at using the general sense to unravel text. They are not afraid to make mistakes and self-correct as they work their way through a story.

The first reading can be followed by a second where the children join in and read together. The teacher looks for opportunities to focus attention on the print and to highlight its form and function. They can talk about words; how you need to read louder when the words get bigger; how some words go down the page and not across; how some words are the same, especially 'I' 'a' 'the', etc. Games can be played like: 'Who can count the words on this page? Where is the first/last word?'

This is a deliberate explicit 'modelling' of the reading process aimed at developing pupils' understanding of the features of language. We saw how some pupils, like Kevin, often come to school knowing very little about 'the nature and purpose of written language' (Reid 1966; Downing 1978) and need help in developing concepts of print. The shared reading of stories, especially in enlarged text, helps such children, as we saw earlier, to develop 'cognitive clarity' or in other words 'the clear understanding of both functional and featural concepts of literacy' (Downing 1985, p.43).

Using functional and environmental print

Of course print is not just in books. We are surrounded by printed words on packets, notices, street signs, clothing. Functional and environmental print is 'embedded' in a relevant permanent context which makes sense and it has a potentially powerful part to play in promoting understanding of concepts of literacy.

Children can go on walks around school and 'guess' what certain labels and signs must mean. In the local environment they can look at words and notice that different kinds of writing are used for different purposes. Back in the classroom, the children can collect boxes, cartons, labels, newspapers, in fact anything which has evidence of print being used to convey information. Once they get the idea, they tend to spot words everywhere and are especially delighted if they arrive at school wearing T-shirts or dresses bearing the same message, whether it be 'Thomas the Tank Engine' or 'Postman Pat'.

Creating texts

Class book-making

It is important with a real-book approach to integrate reading and writing. The children can become 'authors' and write for different audiences using their own language and experiences.

This 'language experience' approach begins simply with labels and messages around the classroom. It can become a collaborative shared-writing process with the children helping to decide on the message and watching as it is written in front of them. Again explicit talk can be used to focus attention on the features of print.

Other kinds of texts can be created: scripts for assembly plays, messages to teachers or parents and big books like the ones used in shared-reading sessions. After reading a particularly good story the children might suggest that they make a book like that! It could involve retelling a story, changing and extending a story or creating a new one. The value of this kind of experience is shown in Figure 3.9.

BOOK-MAKING:

- Provides a context for focusing on aspects of print
- Develops an understanding of the nature and use of print
- Allows the teacher to 'model' the reading and writing process
- Provides opportunities for children to work together to produce a story
- Develops a 'sense of ownership'
- Encourages a strong emotional response to text
- Makes rereading of familiar texts highly likely
- Develops reading skills and strategies
  (prediction, use of pictures, use of rhyme/rhythm, recognition of sight vocabulary)
- Encourages understanding of the world of books; how they are made; and what it means to be an author and illustrator
- Builds a store of known texts
- Integrates all four areas of language (talking, listening, reading, writing)
- Builds up a class library of collaborative texts

Figure 3.9   The benefits of class book-making

Figure 3.10   Class book-making

Individual Book-making

Very young children can begin to make little books based on their own interests and experiences. Goddard (1974) urged that early experience with reading and

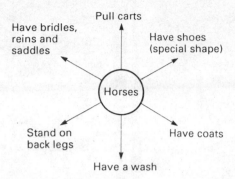

WHAT CLARE KNOWS A LOT ABOUT

Figure 3.11 A brainstorming web

writing should be linked with the child's own preoccupations and give expression to his/her own thoughts, feelings and experiences. Similarly, van Lierop (1985, p.74) believes that if booklets are made which

> centre on children's own activities they are highly motivated to read them. If the wording is generated by the children, it will reflect their own language, be easily predictable and have high interest value.

One way of starting is to ask children if there is something they know a lot about? 'Are they an expert on something?' 'Do they have a special interest?' Claire (age 6) was interested in horses. Her teacher used a brainstorming web to record what she knew (Figure 3.11).

The 'web' helped her organize her thinking and plan out the sequence for her book. She was encouraged to write her own version first and then redraft. Extracts from Claire's information book follow on page 52 (Figure 3.12).

Encouraging children to 'have a go' at writing unaided not only recognizes the importance of risk taking and making mistakes in the learning process; it acts as a kind of 'window' whereby the teacher can see what the child knows and understands about print. This diagnostic information can be used to plan future intervention strategies which will help the individual pupil to develop increasing control over the written forms of language. Collecting samples of unaided writing over a period of time also offers the teacher opportunities to develop a deeper understanding of the different stages of the natural writing process.

In the example on pages 54–5 a 7-year-old boy has mapped out his own web and has written each episode without redrafting (Figure 3.15).

We can see how he is very aware of writing for an audience; he has powerful insight into the part played by illustration in conveying meaning and has a good grasp of many conventions of print. He does, however, overgeneralize many phonic rules (e.g. mail; dide; maet) and could be helped in this direction. His writing is undoubtedly 'vigorous, committed, honest and interesting' (*English for*

Figure 3.12 Three extracts from Claire's book on horses

Ages 5–11, 10.19) and illustrates how children, 'given the opportunity to use what they know, are able to demonstrate considerable knowledge of the forms and purposes of writing' (10.12).

So, to summarize at this point, individual book-making can play a crucial part in literacy development.

INDIVIDUAL BOOK-MAKING:

- Provides a purposeful, meaningful, relevant reading/writing activity – motivation
- Allows children to become their own experts and show their knowledge and expertise to others
- Develops pupils' sense of power and status
- Creates a positive, valuing classroom ethos
- Develops intellectual abilities
  (children need to order, shape, sequence, structure)
- Develops a sense of writing for an audience
- Provides opportunities for the teacher to learn about the individual child
  (interests/character/abilities)
- Allows the teacher to use individualized teaching strategies and teach literacy skills in the meaningful context of child's own language
- Can develop an apprenticeship approach – the child learning by working alongside a craftsman

---

Figure 3.13   The value of individual book-making

Figure 3.14   Individual book-making

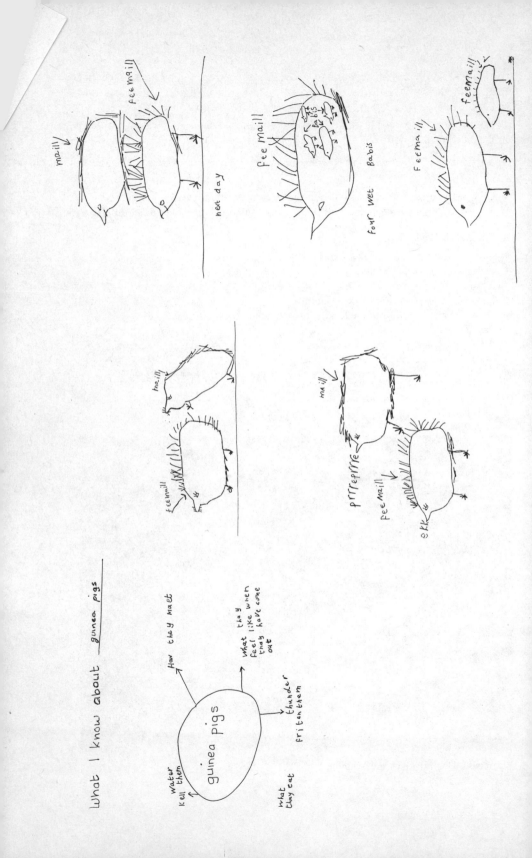

What I know about guinea pigs

How they mait

what they feel like when they have come out

thunder friten them

guinea pigs

water kill them

what they eat

maill

feemaill

hot day

fee maill

four wet babis

Feemaill

feemaill

maill

feemaill

prrreprrre

Feemaill

ekk

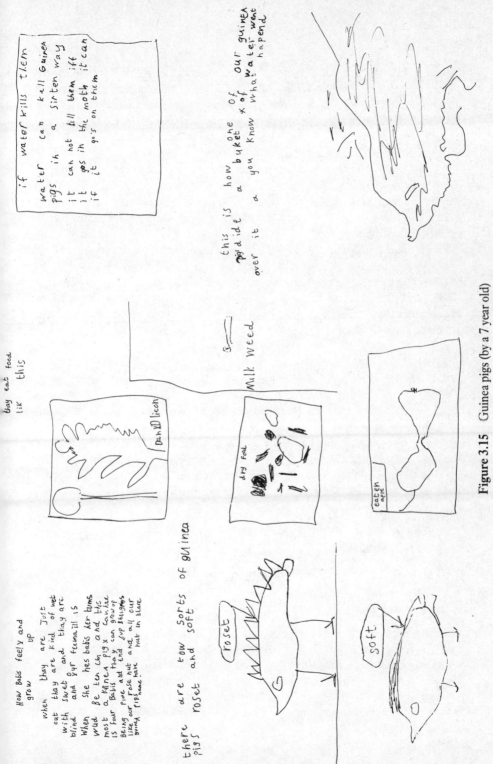

Figure 3.15 Guinea pigs (by a 7 year old)

The role of the child

Taking a closer look

Frequent reading and rereading of stories soon means that the class will develop a store of highly familiar texts. Once children feel they 'know' a story they begin to say, like Kevin before them, that 'This one's easy for me' or 'I can read this' and they then set out to prove to themselves, friends, teachers and parents that they *can* do it, they *can* read. They find learning to read easy because they know the story beforehand. They cannot fail!

It all sounds wonderful and of course it is. It makes learning to read easy. Frank Smith affirms that beginning readers *do* have this one overriding need for learning to read to be made easy (Smith 1978b). Unfortunately, teachers and parents can fear that this is not 'real reading': 'it's only memorizing'; 'they're not learning the words'.

There are a number of things we can do which might help everyone at this stage. We can develop a better understanding of the reading process in order to make sense of what is happening when beginners use 'memory' to recall texts; we can highlight the value and purpose of written language and focus attention on print in the ways discussed earlier; we can allow *time* for the beginner to practise and make sense of reading.

Understanding the natural reading process

Don Holdaway in *The Foundation of Literacy* (1979) uses the bed-time story to illustrate the natural pre-school literacy learning cycle. The young child listens to the stories, asks for them to be repeated, returns voluntarily to the text and gradually by a process of successive approximation begins to match his or her version to the original. The same process appears to be at work when children learn to read with 'real books'. What seems to happen is that the child gets the story right first and then in time, begins to match the story 'in the head' to the words on the page. We see Kevin involved in this process as he reads *The Friend* by John Burningham. The text reads:

> And stay inside when it is raining
> Then I'm by myself.

But Kevin reconstructs the meaning thus:

> When it's raining we stay inside
> now I'm on my own.

After a period of about two weeks and frequent 'reading together' sessions, Kevin's version came closer and closer to the original until it matched.

Of course the most reassuring sign of all *is* when children do break through to the next stage where they rely less and less on memory as they read and use different behaviours with text. Now the natural pattern emerges and the 'memory' stage becomes one very important stepping stone towards independence.

Figure 3.16   Reading – a shared sociable activity

Time for practice

Stories excite children's interest and make them want to try to read them again for themselves. The teacher's role now changes to that of provider of time and opportunities for the kinds of self-directed, self-generated reading behaviour characteristic of the young fluent reader. The children need to 'programme' themselves and make sense of reading in their own way and at their own pace, they need time to puzzle things out for themselves and learn to read by reading.

Children can reread the familiar stories of the big books in enlarged text or use the smaller versions of resources such as *Story Chest* (Arnold Wheaton 1982). Self-made books always develop a strong sense of ownership and consequently children return to them over and over again; their repetitive, rhythmical language structures offer support in reconstructing meaning: 'What do you like? I like bacon. What do you like? I like chips.' Most children have a repertoire of known songs and rhymes. Such texts are ideal for the beginner, their rhythmical qualities encouraging anticipation and prediction and the matching of the 'story in the head' to the words on the page. It seems that a number of children do teach themselves to read by reading and rereading nursery rhymes, until they achieve an accurate word–sound match.

Later on, when children have had many experiences of sharing stories in this way their behaviour starts to change as they begin to pick out known sight words in the book; to recite the text, accurately matching spoken words with text by pointing with a finger. Here the adult continues to encourage the reader to be a problem solver and to puzzle things out using previously learnt strategies. Guessing at unknown words is encouraged through questions like: 'What makes sense? What might fit? What could it be? Does that sound right?'

Shared-reading experiences give children the message that learning to read is enjoyable, purposeful and meaningful. They find out at the very beginning that books are worthwhile and have an important part to play in their lives. Shared-reading encourages positive attitudes; the reading and enjoyment of the stories is seen as its own reward. There is no hint of competition or the need for extrinsic reward; no need to 'please Mummy or teacher' or to 'get on to a higher book'. Sharing stories in this way emphasizes that reading is a sociable activity, for when children read exciting stories they want to share what they have found with others. Even the quietest child is stimulated to talk, to express feelings and ideas.

Conclusions

This chapter began with a case study of Kevin (6), a child whose difficulties in learning to read were primarily the result of a mismatch between his needs and the teacher's programme of reading. Reducing and fragmenting language for pupils like Kevin, who have had fewer opportunities to engage in meaningful literacy events, can present considerable problems in learning to read, simply because children fail to make sense of it all. The most significant effect is to remove reading from the needs, experiences and interests of individual children, with the result that pupils become passive learners within a narrow, restricted irrelevant programme.

The alternative shared-reading approach, using 'real books' which treat language as an integrated whole and which create a natural context for literacy development like that of the literate home, was able to reflect Kevin's need for reading to be less stressful, more meaningful and more purposeful. It made him feel that, at last, there was something in reading for him.

This chapter has suggested how a developmental model of reading and language learning, which recognizes and caters for diverse abilities and backgrounds, can begin to be translated into classroom practice. The teacher helps by acting as guide, facilitator, modeller and supporter; and the child learns through problem solving, hypothesizing and trial and error.

This model for the teaching and learning of reading is similar to that of successful language learning at home. The child is 'immersed' in language, listens to it, makes sense of it and gradually joins in, getting better and better at it with time and practice.

It is this model which provides continuing support for all pupils as they develop insight and understanding and learn to 'read for real'.

Acknowledgements

I would like to thank the following for their practical support and their permission to include examples of work in this chapter: Susan Wain, Carol Brammer, Lesley Hall, Marilyn Phipps and Maureen Bradley.

4 Organizing for reading 7–11

MAURA FITZPATRICK

Primary schools must have a clear policy and whole school approach to the teaching of reading which builds success for all children so that they clearly identify themselves as young readers who find pleasure in books. Schools must provide a dynamic reading environment where children are motivated to take their place as readers, encouraged and supported by structured and sensitive teaching.

English for Ages 5–11 (DES 1988a)

In the process of formulating a school policy where it is planned to use the very best of children's literature, both fiction and non-fiction, as the basis for enabling the children 'to identify themselves as young readers who find pleasure in books', the school will encounter some exciting challenges. The requirements of a National Curriculum, the development of teachers' own knowledge, concepts, skills and attitudes to enable them to provide a structured and sensitive learning environment, parental involvement, resourcing, record keeping, and the constant monitoring and evaluation of the language programme are only some of the issues that will be constantly under review and the subject of much formal and informal discussion among teachers. In schools where the climate of professional development is such that teachers can and do interact with and support each other in meeting these challenges, such a language programme can be developed to realize its full potential in terms of the development of both teacher and pupils. In the course of these discussions, the topic of classroom organization is bound to figure very highly. What teachers are concerned with on this issue is simply stated. 'How can I, one teacher with thirty children, manage this approach?'

It must be clear in each teacher's mind that there is not one answer to this question, but many. Just as with any other approach to the teaching and learning of language, there will be as many good systems of classroom organization as there are good teachers. In the course of the implementation of policy, teachers will be constantly learning and relearning, defining and redefining different strategies in managing their programmes not only through their interaction with their colleagues but also with the pupils. Good classroom organization therefore reflects not only the personality of the teacher but also that of the pupils. By definition, then, since the class changes each year, the system of organization will reflect this change in ways that may be subtle and varied, but are significant. This is not a novel idea. All good primary teachers are sensitive to that period of readjustment that takes place during the first half-term of the year when the class and teacher are learning how to manage each other!

However, in the process of developing practice it will become clear that there are certain key elements relating to organization and management of the day-to-day work in the classroom that need to be examined: for example, the physical environment (the classroom and the books available in it), the interlocking relationship between reading and writing, the use of the child's time, the teacher's time and the management of the whole curriculum. It is useful to consider these here in relation to the aims of the school.

Aims and intentions

Good primary practice always depends on a clear statement of aims that enables the teacher to so manage the work in hand that each child will realize these aims as far as he or she is able. It is also in the nature of good innovative practice that teachers can be developing that practice at the same time as they are formulating their aims. In the best school language policies, practice and aims are forming and informing each other and they are interdependent. The saying 'If you don't know where you are going you may end up somewhere else' is certainly true in this context. Since, then, the aims of the language policy, however firmly or tentatively formulated within the school, inform and influence the teacher in the area of classroom organization, they need to be referred to here. We list here some of the aims adopted by one school using good children's literature to promote reading development. We will use these as a reference point in considering the influence of aims on classroom management. Through discussion and reflection on their current practice the school decided:

- that from the very beginning of school life children should develop their confidence in their capacity to read and that they should be encouraged to view themselves as readers regardless of their actual attainment.
- that the children should be encouraged to become voluntary users of books for pleasure, for interest, for information and for that extension of experience and insight that poetry, story and drama can provide.
- that the children should read fluently and with understanding a range of different kinds of material – including their own and their peers' written work – using reading methods appropriate to the material and to the purposes for which they were reading.
- that the children should become critical and discerning readers, able to understand and evaluate the variety of written materials they will meet.
- that the children should develop their sense of audience and purpose.

Organizing resources

How, then, can the physical environment of the classroom be organized so as to enable the child to realize these aims and become a real reader for real purposes? Firstly, there is the question of resources. In deciding what books to use there are several important considerations. Barrie Wade, when he writes 'I would criticize materials of the "See Spot. Run Spot. Run." variety, not only because, as Halliday (1969) says, they bear little relation to the language as a child has learned to use it, but because . . . they turn the food of story into a dry biscuit' reminds all teachers of the critical significance of the quality of the literature they present to the child. This is true whatever stage of development the reader is at, from emergent to fully developed and experienced reader. If our aims are to enable the child to become a critical and discerning reader then we have to accept the responsibility for helping to form tastes in literature. Chapters 6 and 9 of the Cox Report (DES 1988a) indicate clearly the types of reading materials that are the basis of good classroom practice. The books we present to children also serve as models for their own written work, so they should not be required to spend time and energy in the early stages of reading on banal, unproductive texts with little or no narrative content. The initial selection and organization of the books in the classroom is time consuming, so in the junior classes include the children in this work as part of the process of enabling them to become critical, discerning readers. They need to learn that there are few hard and fast rules to be followed, rather that 'good taste' is based on the experience of reading widely and being able to use this experience to make informed judgements. Sometimes a few well chosen comments in the course of reading to the children, be it story, science, maths or any other area of the curriculum, raises the children's awareness that it is a perfectly valid experience to be critical of what they read, be it on the basis of style, content or any other criterion. Comments like 'I think that this is badly/well written because. . . .' from the teacher about a piece of text will encourage children to develop their capacity to become critics of their own written work.

In an ideal world the teacher using this approach to the development of reading would be able to choose a selection of books to suit pupils' needs from the best of the genre. However, given the normal constraints of finance, this is rarely possible. It will be more likely that initially the teacher will have to select from the books already available in the school. In the area of fiction there will probably be some good titles written by good authors. Any money that becomes available for books can be used to supplement these. Additional books may also be available through bulk loans from the local library. Judicious selection from available reading schemes may yield some books that can also be used if they are good stories well written. A useful rule of thumb is that the story should read well when read aloud.

In the junior classroom there will be children who are independent and experienced readers, who can and do read widely for a whole range of purposes.

There may also be children whose reading skills are not yet well developed and these children will still need to experience organic texts, that is, texts where the pictures and language support the reader. There will also be children at various stages of development within these extremes. How, then, can the books be organized to meet the diverse needs of all pupils? Traditionally they were arranged in levels of difficulty and although sometimes the child was allowed to choose within a level she or he might not have been encouraged to choose from the levels above and below the level she or he was 'on'. This is an artificial arrangement and there are alternative systems of organizing books which allow the child to behave more like a 'real' reader.

The children can organize the books according to their own and the teacher's categories. These may be simply fiction and non-fiction, hard-back and paper-back, prose and poetry, adventure stories, etc. Within these categories they may be arranged in ways that are constantly changing. For example, the range of topics covered in the course of the year will lead to the books related to the topic work being heavily read, so these will be chosen according to the theme. Again, the teacher may stimulate interest in many different authors or illustrators in the course of the year and this will naturally generate different arrangements of books.

This is the kind of good practice that can be seen in many classrooms regardless of the approach to reading development that is being used. The significant difference in the approach under discussion is that teaching children how to choose books to meet their own needs is considered to be an intrinsic part of the process of reading development. Choosing is part of the business of taking responsibility for one's own reading. Choice will mean different things for different children and to manage book selection well the teacher needs to know what stage in the reading process each child is at, the next stage in the reading process that it is necessary to experience and what books are available that will meet these needs. This is not as demanding as it sounds, because teachers who can develop high quality interaction with their pupils through sensitive intervention, discussion and shared-reading activities also learn very quickly about the reading process and soon become their own experts. The teacher will also have to be a reader and learn about the books, as different types of books have different qualities.

In the course of teaching the child to choose well the teacher also has to remember that each individual will have a range of needs. For example, the less well developed readers in the junior class, besides needing a wide experience of organic texts to support the development of cueing strategies at the level at which they could be expected to read with some support, also need to have access to levels above and below this. Books that are easier in terms of difficulty of text help to consolidate strategies already learned and provide a feeling of mastery, while access to books of a greater level of difficulty of text not only serves to encourage a love of story and keeps readers highly motivated during this stage of development, but also provides experience of the richness of the syntactic and semantic properties of the language that serve as models in their own language development. A child needs to get this kind of language 'on his ear'.

How access to texts at this level is to be managed will be looked at later when we consider the organization of the child's and the teacher's time. Some children instinctively choose well in the classroom and library. For others, advising them (not making choices for them) and ensuring that the range of books they choose really does meet all their needs is the responsibility of the teacher. While developed readers may be reading independently from a wide range of texts, the teacher may wish to support the less developed readers in a different way. It may be more appropriate to encourage them to have a small repertoire of books at various levels and for different purposes, and these will be judiciously added to as their experience grows. The point is that 'real' readers do not choose their reading matter in a random, casual or haphazard way; their choice is carefully made in a reflective, considered manner and learning to choose well is an important part of the reading process.

Reading and writing

Reading, of course, is only one of the four modes of language: reading, writing, listening and talking. In terms of language development these modes are completely interdependent and the development of one supports the development of the others. Recognition of this fact underpins the success of the 'reading with real books' approach and the management of the classroom itself needs to reflect this. The furniture needs to be so arranged as to allow children to talk and listen to each other with ease, so that they may be 'real talkers' and 'real listeners', talking and listening for real purposes. The variety of purposes for which they need to talk or read or write or listen all need to be easily accommodated. Arrangements of furniture need to be as flexible as the physical constraints allow. Easy access to tape-recorders and blank tapes is essential. Ideally every classroom should be equipped with a listening centre, headsets and sets of tapes and matching books to facilitate group listening to stories.

Grouping of children also requires careful management. Teachers need to ensure that group work, when they consider it to be appropriate, should actually be group work, not simply an arrangement of furniture in which children work as individuals. The reason for group work is to enable the children to collaborate in ways that actually support their development. At times the teacher will need to know that a group or groups can, by supporting each other, work independently. The teacher is thus freed for more intensive work with other groups or individuals. It is sometimes useful to think in terms of 'high guidance' and 'low guidance' groups. In the course of this type of class management the children will need to learn that there will be times when the teacher is available to support learning, while at other times they will need to find support within a group. Similarly, giving a child the opportunity to explicate tasks in hand to and for other children must not be undervalued in terms of promoting that child's development. Good class management, which raises all children's awareness of their capacity to promote their own and other children's learning, is an important factor in enabling the best possible use to be made of both pupil and teacher time.

Many children have high expectations of their own literacy skills. They come to school believing they are readers and writers and in the early years writing and reading develop together. As children become aware of the different authors who are writing for them, their concept of 'authorship' is developed and, sometimes spontaneously by virtue of their own experiences, they take on the role of authors, writing for real readers. If the child is to be enabled to behave as a 'real writer', both in 'public' and 'private' writing, then classroom organization must readily facilitate this. The teacher may provide, for example, blank books already made up that invite the children to write in them, sheets of paper and card that encourage the children to make the books up in various ways to reflect their own purposes.

Besides the books that the children may write for 'publishing' for their own or other classes, it is important – if they are to behave as real writers – that there are books provided for their own personal writing that may be as private as the individual child chooses and from which even the teacher may be excluded! Paper for drafting purposes needs to be provided and this requires some thought, depending on the needs and purposes of both teacher and child. All children need to understand that writing can be public and 'published'. They also need to understand that it can also be ephemeral, temporary and disposable, that it can either be a definitive expression of what they know or what they want to say at any given moment or that it may represent a tentative exploratory venture into areas of knowledge or feeling that are to be clarified in the process of writing.

Most children are familiar with the idea, 'I write what I know'. The experience of writing in order to learn also has to be provided for in the classroom. The teacher needs to balance the need to keep samples of this type of writing for the purposes of monitoring development and recording achievement with the children's need to know that, if they so choose, a particular piece of writing may be discarded. One useful strategy is to provide cheap pieces of paper that are to be disposed of – computer printout for example – as well as exercise books for the more durable drafts and to include the children in discussions regarding their own and the teacher's needs, thereby resolving the problem by encouraging the children to choose their materials appropriately. The important consideration here is that teachers accept that writing improves by writing and that not all of the child's writing has to be filtered through or mediated by the teacher (while at the same time recognizing that the quality of the teacher–pupil interaction is also critical in the development of the child).

Organizing time

While the management of the teacher's and children's time cannot be considered separately from the school's aims, the resources available and the physical arrangements of the classroom, the key to successful management of time requires the development of an appropriate teaching and learning policy. For a good model of effective teaching and learning we look at the language of the child on entry to school, by which time the normal child has a highly developed, tacit understanding of the linguistic rule system of his mother tongue. Listening carefully to reception class children talking to each other reveals clearly that the syntactical patterns they use follow a recognizable order: for example they know that adjectives normally precede nouns, that the subject normally precedes the object, etc.

The kind of learning that has enabled this to occur is sometimes referred to as developmental learning and it is characterized by a dynamic and highly interactive partnership between adult and child, and child and child, that takes place in an environment that is very supportive of the learner. Don Holdaway, in *Independence in Reading* (1972), describes the important characteristics of this type of learning. Some of these characteristics have significant implications for classroom management. He writes, 'It occurs in an environment in which the mature skill is being used by everyone with obvious functional success'. The child learns to talk because he has a great need to talk and he is surrounded by people who are doing it. In the classroom, therefore, both the teacher and the pupils need to be using the four modes of language 'with obvious functional success'.

This means, for example, that it is good practice for the teacher to ensure that some part of the day is set aside for children and teacher to engage in sustained private reading. Teachers should not underestimate their usefulness as role models for some children both as readers and as writers. Reference was made earlier to the fact that developing readers at every stage need to have access to texts that might normally be considered 'too difficult' or 'too easy' for them. The making of tapes for use in a listening centre facilitates this and provides a use of reading in the junior class that is pleasurable, functional, as well as an economical use of teacher and child time. In one class the taping of '*Story Chest*' (Arnold Wheaton) plays became for a time an absorbing feature of the day's work; but the class might equally well have used non-fiction, perhaps related to topic work, to which the whole class could then have access. These tapes can also be made by recording the normal sessions in which the teacher reads aloud. Children soon learn that during these taping sessions interjections are not appropriate or that they need to make a notice for outside the classroom, 'Recording in progress. Please do not enter'.

Traditionally there has been great emphasis in primary classrooms on teachers listening to children reading. While of course teachers need to listen to children, there needs to be equal emphasis on children listening to teachers while they share the same text. Incidentally, this wider use of teachers as readers also enables them to become their own experts in learning about children's literature and the range of purposes for which different books can be used to promote reading development with different children. These readings of stories, poems, plays and non-fiction with a child or a group of children can be taped to good effect. The normal classroom sounds, within reason, do not have a deleterious effect on the recording and in fact often encourage the diffident reader to read along with the tape because of the impression of being part of the group. In this way a good store of tapes will soon become available that enable individuals or groups to have access to texts *independently of the teacher*.

An approach to reading development known as 'shared reading' can be very easily adapted for classroom use. Besides group and individual reading, children enjoy having their own reading partners. These may be similar or mixed ability partnerships. There is growing body of evidence of the value of shared reading for reading development when the tutor is an adult. When the tutor is another child, however, the tutor-child gains as much as or even more than the friend who is being tutored. Teachers need not be concerned, therefore, that using able readers in this way is in any sense 'wasting their time'. This practice in the classroom is another way of giving access to the more demanding texts that less developed readers require.

Some teachers may be concerned at the suggestion that even the children who are developed readers need to be read to. It helps in the management of time if teachers and pupils together can clear up some of the misapprehensions about what reading aloud entails. In some classrooms children read aloud only when their progress is being checked by the teacher. In these cases, it is hardly surprising that they come to associate reading aloud with 'being tested'. It is patently inefficient to organize reading time on a page-a-day basis for each pupil. Under such a regime young readers can hardly see a purpose other than routine performance or testing. Many read below their best, because it takes time to settle into reading fluently. Reading fragments does not develop enjoyment of narrative. Some children are stopped at the bottom of a page even if it ends in mid-sentence.

Where children and teachers alike have been accustomed to the traditional view of what counts as 'hearing reading', it takes some readjustment to see that hearing reading *from any source* counts as 'hearing reading'. It may be a piece of the child's own written work, or a piece of text from a book being used in the topic; or perhaps during a maths lesson the child may read to the teacher from the maths textbook. These are good functional usages of reading that have not normally enjoyed the status of the 'reading book' for the purposes of hearing the child read. But why not? It is important, however, that the children also realize that reading can be 'heard' in the course of many curricular areas and in a range of contexts, not only to protect the teacher from the cry 'Miss, you haven't heard me read', but also because the child needs to know that the teacher is interested in and involved with every learner's progress. The teacher also needs to know how individual children are developing in their reading in these other curricular areas. After all, the intention is that the children should be real readers for real purposes and their reading progress across the curriculum should be forming part of the teacher's assessment.

Assessment of progress is a major factor related to the use of teacher time since good formative assessment procedures, both formal and informal, are crucial to the success of real reading. It is possible to maximize use of teacher time and demonstrate good functional use of written language by giving this work a high profile in the classroom and engaging the children in some of the record keeping. For example, a class 'Good news book' may be kept, in which all children have their own pages allocated to them. Their positive achievements are recorded in this book by the teacher, who can often involve the child in deciding what has to be written. The book, of course, may be read by anyone in the class – providing the teacher takes care to ensure legibility – and at times it has almost been the most read book in the room.

Children can also be encouraged to select the pieces of written work that are to be used as examples of attainment and can stick them into their own profile book or folder. This is not only a good use of pupils' time; it also provides them with valuable insight into their own development and enables them to develop a sense of shared ownership of the record-keeping system with the teacher, which is sometimes helpful as a positive, motivating factor.

Most teachers are familiar with the idea of junior age children keeping their own reading diaries. An extension of this which provides a context for purposeful, relevant and functional use of all four language modes is to have the children keep a simple log of work in progress. When, for example, introducing a new topic, the teacher might map out on the blackboard her view of how the work might progress. Through discussion this outline will probably be amended to include the children's ideas. This plan might be photocopied and given to each child as the start of the log, on the clear understanding that it will be constantly amended. Without ever abdicating professional responsibility it is possible to involve the children in making decisions about, for example, what written work is to be completed and when, and encouraging them to keep a log of work completed. Similarly the teacher might discuss 'targets' at group level and appoint a member of the group to monitor progress. Initially, none of this may be done very expertly by the children but, if established, the initial time spent on encouraging evaluation and constructive criticism by the teacher will be rewarded by having several children who enjoy and respond to the challenge of having at least some ownership of the management of their work – useful allies for a busy teacher (see Figure 4.1).

When giving the children some ownership of their work is combined with tasks that the children see as both relevant and purposeful, junior age children do, in fact, make effective decisions and organize themselves well. For example, if they are making a book to be read by others, the children themselves will make the decision regarding whether or not a particular piece of handwriting is good enough to be included or whether it needs to be rewritten. Again, if one or two children decide they will tape a book, they will often be observed engaging in rigorous practice which is self-motivated, especially if the book chosen is more difficult than they would normally be asked to read independently. Good, sensitive and innovative class teachers can devise many such strategies that encourage the children to operate both independently and effectively in the classroom.

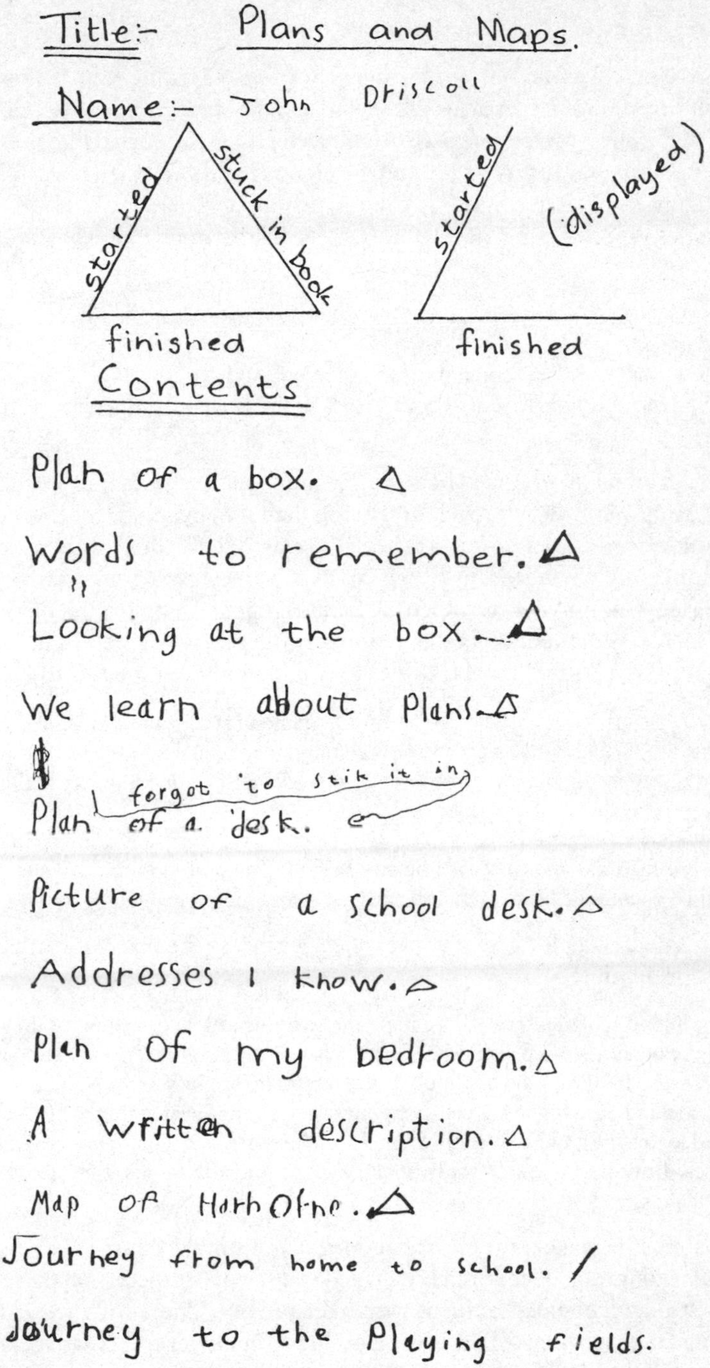

Title:-   Plans and Maps.

Name:- John Driscoll

started   stuck in book   started   (displayed)

finished   finished

Contents

Plan of a box. △

Words to remember. △

Looking at the box. △

We learn about Plans. △

Plan̶ ̶of̶ ̶a̶ ̶desk̶. (I forgot to stik it in)

Picture of a school desk. △

Addresses I know. △

Plan of my bedroom. △

A written description. △

Map of Hothorne. △

Journey from home to school. /

Journey to the Playing fields.

Figure 4.1 John, aged 7, example of log of work on the topic 'Plans and maps'

Organizing for the whole curriculum

Clearly the practices of self-motivation, choosing, deciding and taking some responsibility for evaluation of progress, which have been discussed in relation to an effective policy for reading, also have relevance for managing the whole curriculum. If they are encouraged and developed in this way then reading will be perceived as a natural way of learning, not as a separated skill. A recent mathematics report (DES 1988c), for example, listed among 'personal qualities' (7.13):

> perseverance, reliability and accuracy in working through a sequence of stages in an extended text;
> willingness to check, monitor and control their own work;
> independence of thought and action as well as the ability to co-operate within a group.

The management of the whole curriculum may be less problematic for teachers using a holistic approach to reading than for any other. In the course of developing whole-school policies, especially related to the delivery of a National Curriculum, thought needs to be given to the question of how far a cross-curricular approach to delivery needs to be developed. An indication of the need for this considered attention is, for example, Attainment Target 19 in a recent Science Working Party Report (DES 1988d) which states, for age 7 to 11,

> On the basis of work carried out in the programme of study children should have opportunity further to develop and use communication skills in presenting their ideas and reporting their work to a range of audiences including other children, teachers, parents and other adults.
> They should be helped to consider and use methods of communication appropriate to the material and to the audience. In both oral and written accounts they should be encouraged to present information in an ordered manner.

The Mathematics report is also very explicit regarding the place of maths in the overall curriculum (10.33).

> In drawing up schemes of work we hope that schools will take account of the part which mathematics can play in whole experience of the pupil at school. Mathematics certainly should not be confined to the 'mathematics lesson': it is a tool to be developed and used in most areas. It is generally well appreciated that mathematics is needed by the pupils to help them to understand and communicate in the sciences. But other areas of study, including the arts and humanities, also need mathematics.

These statements make quite clear that, for example, in the course of a session in which a class or group of children is engaged in a science project, that there could well be a strong mathematical focus within the project. There will most certainly be a strong language focus. This is not a problem, but in terms of management of a National Curriculum it will be essential for the teacher to be very aware that, in the example quoted, three areas of the curriculum are being covered. Good

MY JOURNEY

I open my door. I walk straight a head. I get into my car and I am off. I turn right I go straight ahead to the top of Poole Crescent.

I cross the Quinton Road into Mill Farm Road. We go up Mill Farm Road, past the Park. Then we come to Grove Lane. We go to the shop. Then back to the car, and carry on to Old Church Road. When we get to the top we turn right we go along Old Church Road until we meet Harborne Park Road. We turn left, we carry on up Harborne Park. It is a dual carriage way. We turn right just after the traffic lights into Vivian Road and then right again into Vivian Close where we park the car and I walk past the Church and down the drive to School.

By
DAVID WALSH

Junior One.

Figure 4.2   David, aged 8, example of work on map reading

language teachers who are trying to develop 'real readers' who read for 'real purposes' are those teachers who are aware of the possibility for language development that exists across the curriculum and who can exploit this to the advantage of the child.

In Figure 4.2 David shows that he has learned precision of language in the course of developing his map-reading skills. He uses the computer to produce his final draft. In Figure 4.3 Emma, aged 10, shows how she has integrated historical information with her own knowledge about shopping.

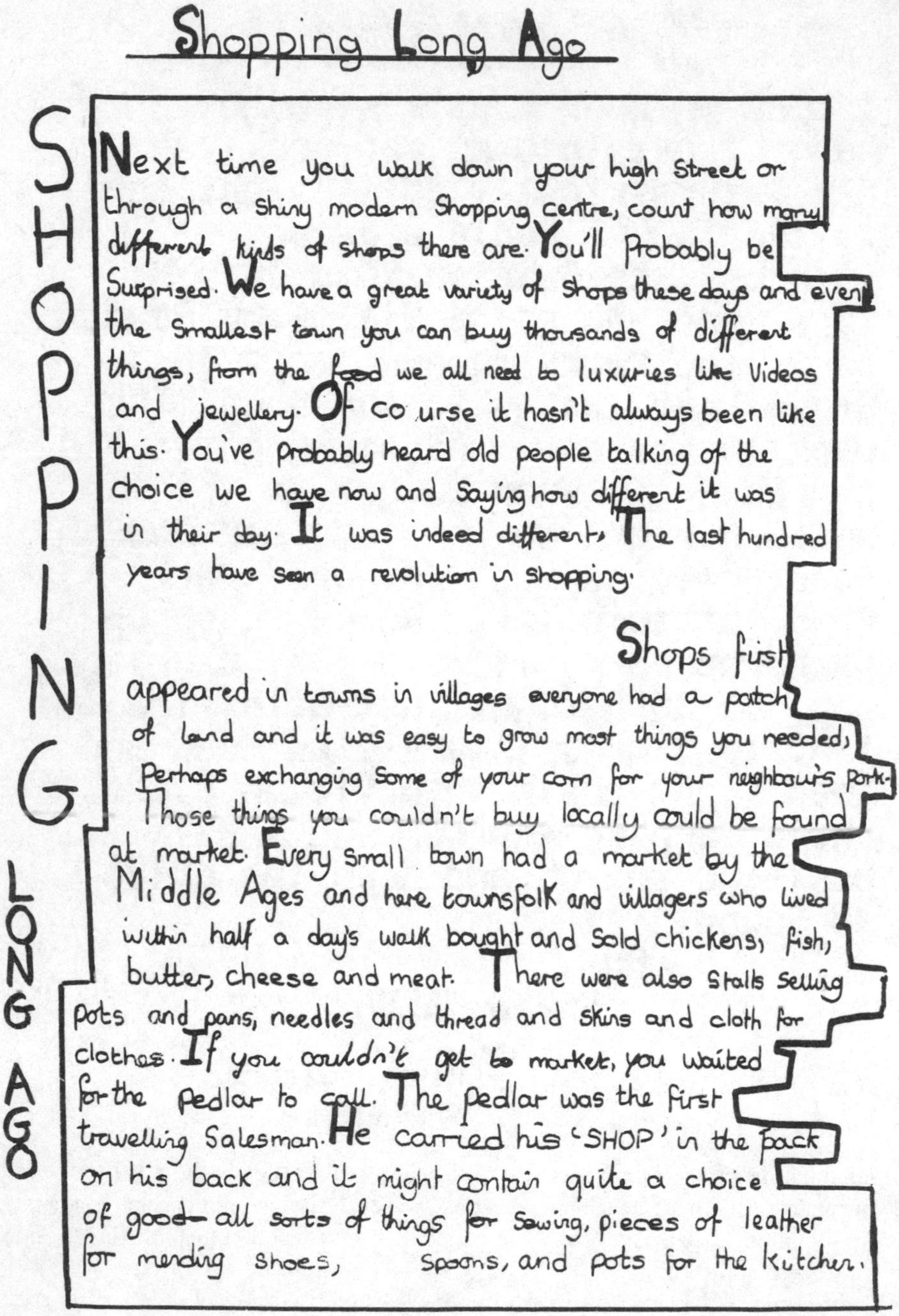

Shopping Long Ago

SHOPPING

LONG AGO

Next time you walk down your high street or through a shiny modern shopping centre, count how many different kinds of shops there are. **Y**ou'll probably be surprised. **W**e have a great variety of shops these days and even the smallest town you can buy thousands of different things, from the food we all need to luxuries like videos and jewellery. **O**f course it hasn't always been like this. **Y**ou've probably heard old people talking of the choice we have now and saying how different it was in their day. **I**t was indeed different. **T**he last hundred years have seen a revolution in shopping.

Shops first appeared in towns in villages everyone had a patch of land and it was easy to grow most things you needed, perhaps exchanging some of your corn for your neighbour's pork. **T**hose things you couldn't buy locally could be found at market. **E**very small town had a market by the **M**iddle **A**ges and here townsfolk and villagers who lived within half a day's walk bought and sold chickens, fish, butter, cheese and meat. **T**here were also stalls selling pots and pans, needles and thread and skins and cloth for clothes. **I**f you couldn't get to market, you waited for the pedlar to call. **T**he pedlar was the first travelling salesman. **H**e carried his 'SHOP' in the pack on his back and it might contain quite a choice of good— all sorts of things for sewing, pieces of leather for mending shoes,   spoons, and pots for the kitchen.

Figure 4.3   Emma, aged 10, example of writing in a history topic

At the heart of good classroom management is the effective teacher. Teachers using real books successfully in the classroom will be teachers who develop their own style of management that recognizes and meets both their own and their pupils' needs. Although by definition this will mean that a variety of systems of management will emerge even within one school – and that is good – effective teachers will have certain characteristics in common. These will include the willingness to interact with colleagues and to share successes and mistakes in terms of both developing and managing the approach, a willingness to take risks, to learn from 'mistakes' and to encourage pupils to do the same. They will know that the best way to become their own experts in the approach is to observe children sensitively, to learn from this observation and to apply the knowledge gained. They will view their role in the classroom mainly, though not necessarily exclusively, as facilitators and enablers. They will know of and be able to use a range of teaching styles, with those balanced and flexible approaches that are so essential to help develop the child's knowledge, concepts and skills and attitudes throughout his/her literacy programme. They will know how to help children to apply these gains in developing themselves as language users and as learners across the curriculum. They will be skilful managers of children, able to organize them to work individually, in pairs, in groups or as a class as the need arises.

English for Ages 5–11 (DES 1988a) refers directly to an earlier report, affirming the centrality of the learner:

> At the heart of the educational process lies the child. No advances in policy, no acquisitions of new equipment have their desired effect unless they are in harmony with the nature of the child.

> CACE 1967, 1.2.9

Teachers might also ponder on the need to develop systems of classroom management and organization that are in harmony with their own natures; and as they reflect on the requirements of their own children and their capacity to respond to all needs, they will, above all, need to be confident in their ability to be fair to themselves.

PART THREE
Resources and support

5 Support for real reading

CHRIS BURMAN

Parent–teacher partnership

The role of parents in the education of their children has continued to gather momentum ever since the Plowden Committee (DES 1967) showed that of the factors influencing a child's performance the interest of parents must be placed first and foremost. Eight years later the Bullock Report stated emphatically 'there is no doubt whatsoever of the value of parents' involvement in the early stages of reading' and more recently the Cox Report *English for Ages 5–11* (DES 1988a) has gone further in suggesting that 'teachers need to organise the learning in ways which follow on logically and consistently from the successful language learning which children have already accomplished in the context of their own homes and communities' (2.5).

The benefit to parents

Evidence continues to show that when homes and schools develop positive and supportive partnerships, all three parties – teachers, parents and pupils – stand to benefit. Parents develop confidence when they realize the importance of their own contributions and when they know that their efforts are recognized and valued. If they can become active participants, they are able to take an important role in supporting their child's education; they can provide a happy, secure learning environment and use their knowledge of their child to relate reading to their particular interests. This can develop a better parental understanding of the process of reading and an increased ability to recognize progress and achievement.

The benefit to teachers

Teachers, in turn, can capitalize on what parents have to offer. However busy, parents can give more time than the teacher in a class of 30. They can provide many more opportunities for the sharing of stories than the teacher alone.

Children need far more help with reading than teachers can provide, if they are to become 'real' readers, that is children who not only *can* read but *do* read for meaning and pleasure (Bennett 1979). If teachers can encourage a shared commitment to the success of the individual child and create an atmosphere of openness, honesty and understanding, they will be in a much better position to advise and inform parents on the natural reading process, the stages of reading behaviour development and how parents can help at home. Parents need to understand that good readers guess at words they do not know and use sense to work their way through a text. They need to understand that contrary methods used at home like look-and-say or phonics could undermine the child's confidence and affect progress.

Similarly, parents will need to know that in the early stages children will rely heavily on memory to retell stories and that this is a strategy to be encouraged and praised. So the more opportunities available for explanation of the different stages of development, the less likely are parents to give children the message that 'it's not really reading'.

Teachers will also need to encourage parents to recognize the respective duality and compatibility of their roles in helping children achieve literacy. Some parents may not realize that what they often do instinctively and intuitively at home, reading and sharing stories and modelling literacy in use, is what teachers are seeking to re-create in school (see Chapter 3). So when teachers recognize the vital contribution of parents and when parents see and appreciate what teachers are doing to help their child at school, there is far less room for criticism, misunderstanding and suspicion.

The benefits to pupils

Pupils undoubtedly benefit when they know that teachers and parents are in broad agreement about aims and objectives and are working together in their best interest. As parents and teachers work towards common goals the child is far more likely to see a connection between the two worlds of school and home and to perceive school learning as an extension of the home experience and the family relationship. Reading becomes part of daily home life, a natural shared family activity and not just something that happens in school.

Successful home–school partnerships are particularly important in the very beginning stages of reading when children are developing confidence in them-selves and are starting to take on a view of what reading is all about. They need to find learning to read easy and within their reach. They need to work with familiar texts which offer support at many different levels. They need a lot of time to practise. While opportunities can be provided at school for the repetition of familiar stories, the more the parent can share known texts the more quickly the child will be able to develop important reading strategies which will bring success.

Parental involvement in education is important, decisively so, for educational success. In the case of reading, the relationship between pupil success and encouragement from home is clear and overwhelmingly supported by investigation and evidence. Esnouf (1983) said 'we must take parents profoundly into our confidence and find ways of working together with parents raised to the level of active participants'. Success with a real-book or shared-reading approach depends on such involvement. Schools need to gain parents' confidence, enlist their support and develop understanding of what they are doing, how they are doing it and how parents can help. Different schools will need to identify all the ways and means by which this can be achieved, taking account of the existing pattern of home–school links, the nature of the catchment area and the age group involved. Different ways of informing different sets of parents will need to be explored. What follows is an account of one infant school's attempts to utilize the expertise and willingness of parents as partners. The nature of that involvement ranges from parents' meetings, reading booklets and guidelines, parents helping at school, home reading notebooks and informal conversations between parents and teachers. Not all the strategies were equally successful, but each initiative provided parents with the *opportunity* to participate in their own child's education.

Parents' meetings

The first meeting

An invitation was extended to all parents to attend either an afternoon or evening meeting at which the head and staff could explain why they felt there was a need for change, why they believed a story-based approach was a better way for children to learn to read and what shared reading involved at home and at school. It began with a review of the reading books already in use, many of which were outdated, included racial, cultural, gender stereotypes, had little or no story line and used artificial disjointed patterns of language. The headteacher attempted to raise parental awareness that such texts could promote negative attitudes to reading in that those pupils who *could* read might choose *not* to read; others might read for the wrong reasons; to 'get on to a higher book' or 'please Mummy'. For comparison, story books like *Not Now Bernard* (David McKee) or *Hairy Bear* (*Story Chest*: Arnold Wheaton) were read aloud to parents in an attempt to show that such stories help to produce real readers who read for pleasure and meaning and see reading as *thinking*.

The shared-reading approach was explained using a professional video and reassuring evidence was given that where parents have been interested and involved in sharing books with their children regularly, their reading performance had improved dramatically. The overriding message given to parents was 'We need you. We need you to spend *time* reading with your child so that she or he will become a *real* reader, one who feels that books *matter* and that reading is worthwhile.'

The meeting ended with an opportunity for parents to look at the new reading

SO WHY STORIES?

We think that there are six main reasons why children should use real story books from the beginning.

1 *Stories help to excite children's interest in reading*
Children must want to become readers. When they hear a good story read aloud, they will often try to read it again for themselves. So stories are what attracts them to wanting to learn to read in the first place.

2 *Stories meet children's emotional needs*
Small children are all the time trying to make sense of the world around them; stories dealing with familiar everyday situations like family outings, parties or holidays provide security and reassurance. Also stories which deal with possibly worrying situations, getting lost, the dark, monsters etc. help children come to terms with their own fears. Stories dealing with emotions like love, anger, jealousy and many more, help children understand their own feelings and perhaps why others behave as they do. All this helps a child's development.

3 *Stories give children the message that learning to read is enjoyable, purposeful and meaningful*
We believe that the way children learn to read affects their whole attitude to reading and to books in the future. If children find out at the very beginning, that books are worthwhile, then they are far more likely to read for pleasure later on.

4 *Real stories encourage a positive attitude to reading*
We see reading and the enjoyment of story as its own reward. We do not want children to 'read for the race' or to get on to a 'higher book' or to please Mummy.

5 *Stories encourage talk and thinking*
When children read exciting story books they will often want to share what they find in the story with others. This excitement stimulates even the quietest child to talk, to express feelings and ideas. All this helps language development.
   You will probably find that when children become involved in stories they will start to discuss the pictures, the characters and the things that happen. Often they will link this to their own experience. This helps them to think but it is a special kind of thinking which will help in the learning of other school subjects later on.

6 *Learning to read with stories – the natural way to learn*
Most of the things children, and indeed all of us learn to do, we learn by trying the whole thing out first and then gradually, through practice, trial and error, we get better and better at it. Think of walking, talking, swimming, driving etc. . . .
   We see reading as learned in the same way. Children learn by recognizing that pictures tell a story, a story they can laugh about, talk about, enjoy. Gradually they interpret the print a little at a time and finally can read and enjoy story books, can read and obtain facts from information books.

Figure 5.1   Information for parents on the value of story

material; Kaleidoscope collections of picture books, *Story Chest* books and tapes, parents' handbooks and a library loan of fiction and non-fiction including poetry, nursery rhymes, plays etc.

The second meeting

After a term parents were again invited into school to become involved in and aware of what was happening with the teaching of reading. The focus to begin with was again on the *why*: why stories? Why natural reading methods? Why should parents help?

More emphasis was placed on the role of stories in addressing children's personal and emotional needs. Recurring themes in picture books like *Titch* and *You'll Soon Grow into Them, Titch* (Pat Hutchins) were used to illustrate how such books help very young children come to terms with powerful emotions like fear, anger, jealousy and loneliness. Staff showed examples of children's talk to show how these deeper layers of meanings within stories encourage even the youngest, quietest children to talk and think, to share ideas and concerns and to make sense of themselves and the world. Information was made available to re-emphasize the role of stories in developing active, creative readers (Figure 5.1).

At this meeting, the natural, whole to part or holistic approach to reading was compared with the way children and all of us learn most of the things we do. We learn by taking on the whole act, by trying it out and getting better and better at the smaller skills in time and with practice (see Waterland 1985). The reading process was linked to the model of oral language learning whereby the child is 'immersed' in language in use; hears it; orders it; makes sense of it and gradually, with support, joins in as more language becomes meaningful.

Parents were encouraged to see themselves as natural teachers of their own children. They had taught them all they could do before they came to school; in particular they had helped them learn to speak. The message was 'don't stop now and simply hand over to professionals'. Children do better at school when parents and teachers work *together*. Again, a booklet was used to reinforce the need for parental involvement and what parents can do to help at each stage. The booklet (1) is illustrated here in its entirety.

Different kinds of shared reading opportunities were filmed: teacher and child; mother and child; nursery nurse and child; child and child, but in each scene the focus was on the pride and success which comes from reading books together.

Stories were shown being used to develop learning in all curriculum areas including maths, art, language, music and dance. The big *Story Chest* book *The Red Rose* had been used to help consolidate mathematical ideas like colour and sets. *The Monsters' Party* had led to a collage of monsters and related writing and reading activities. In another class a theme on transport had originated from *To Town* and had led to art work, model making, experiences of solid shapes and the writing of personal imaginative stories on 'when I go to town'.

BOOKLET 1

AT HOME

WHY SHOULD YOU HELP ?

1   <u>You</u> are your child's natural teacher. <u>You</u> helped your child
         eat, walk, dress, talk - don't stop now that s/he has started
         school. Your child needs to be <u>prepared</u> for learning to
         read and you are the best person to begin this preparation.

2   Children need far more help with reading than teachers
         alone can provide if they are to become real readers.

3   Children do better at school when parents and teachers work
         together

4   The sharing of a book and its stories can bring you and
         your child closer together.

Which books ?

Children will be given a choice from a range of short, amusing and well
illustrated story books. They are more <u>eager</u> to read when given this
freedom and their choice should be respected.
They may choose a book that seems very easy. Don't worry. That book will
build confidence and make them feel successful. The important thing is
that the child WANTS to read the books.

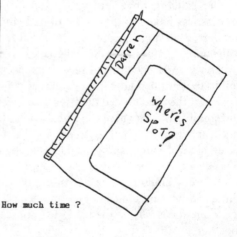

How much time ?

Little   and often is best. Make this a quiet, peaceful and comfy
time, free from distractions. Keep the sessions short and fun.

|

1   WHAT DO YOU DO ?

A   Talk about the book

Read the title. Talk about what might happen in the story - your
child is learning to predict - a very important skill in reading.
Talk about the pictures, they also tell the story. Use questions like

"What is happening here ?"
"What can you see ?"
"Why do you think ?"
"How will they feel ?"

mum
and
claire

B   Read together

Make sure your child can see the print and the pictures.
Show where to start the story and how to turn the pages.
Read the story together. Point to the words as you read
them, pointing helps children match what they say with the words on
the page.
Don't stop to try to build up the words, keep the flow of the story.
Talk about the pictures - later children need to use the pictures
to   help them work out new words on a page.
Read and re-read the story if your child wants to hear it.
Let your child 'read' the story to you afterwards, even if this is
reciting by heart or making up the story from the pictures.

C   Talk about the book again

This should be a genuine sharing of ideas and opinions. Encourage
your child to talk about his/her own feelings. Did the story or
characters make him/her feel happy, angry, sad ? Hopefully your child
will link what s/he finds in the book with personal real-life
experiences. This is also very important and to be encouraged.

" Zebedee's whiskers
are like a
barbed-wire fence

(-Gemma)

So :-
Read..........listen.............talk.................read.........listen
.........talk...........read............listen.............talk.

2

WHAT NEXT

When they become familiar with the stories they WILL memorise them. Don't worry - this is a stage which cannot be omitted. The children will be trying to read to you even before s/he can read.

ENCOURAGE them and PRAISE their efforts.

Remember

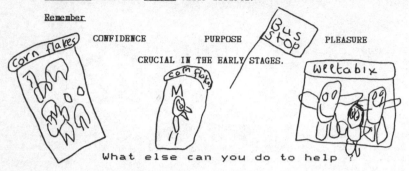

CONFIDENCE   PURPOSE   PLEASURE

CRUCIAL IN THE EARLY STAGES.

What else can you do to help ?

1 Reading is not just books.

We are surrounded by printed words. The more you point out the words on packets, tins, street signs, T.V., in newspapers and comics, the more children will get the message that reading is all around and it is important.
Having fun with print in this way will help your child understand what a 'word' or a 'letter' is in a natural and meaningful way.

2 Read yourself

Show your child that you also find reading enjoyable. If you are seen reading your child will be more likely to do it for him/herself. Children like to imitate grown-ups !

3 Visit the library

Libraries offer the opportunity for browsing and finding books you can share. Help your child to choose and take care of the books.
Look for authors like:- John Burningham, Pat Hutchins, Shirley Hughes, Eric Carle, Eric Hill, their books particularly meet the needs of the beginning reader.

3

2   LATER ON

After your child has had a lot of books read to him/her and has 'shared' many stories with you, the teacher and other children you may find that her/his behaviour begins to change during story sesions. Now you will find your child beginning to pick out words in the book, reciting the text accurately and trying to match the spoken words with the text by pointing with a finger. When your child feels confident s/he will want to read alone. Let her/him do as much as possible, being ready to help when you are asked to.

<u>Remembering these points will help</u>

* Do <u>not</u> help and correct when the child tries <u>unless</u> s/he gets into real difficulties and has obviously lost the <u>sense</u>. <u>Children need to learn to puzzle out text from the sense of the story</u>

* Do not worry if the child's reading is not word perfect.
  <u>Sense</u> is the vital consideration. If the sense has been lost then offer to take over and read the story.

* Do <u>not</u> encourage your child to use phonics (sounds) at this stage. Other reading skills like prediction; using rhythm and rhyme, using the general meaning, using the pictures and the first letter sound are all far more important. S/he will also be beginning to build up a store of words that s/he recognises on sight.

* Do not worry when your child returns to favourite books perhaps time and time again. It builds <u>confidence</u> and encourages the development of the <u>important</u> reading skills.

* Do have <u>fun</u> with the books . You can play word-search games e.g. "Can you find another word like that one ?"
  You can point out the beginning letters and ask "Can you find any other words that start in the same way ?"
  You can enjoy the nonsense words 'bim-bam-bash' 'skiddle-dee-doo' and perhaps make up some together.

* Do remember that reading <u>with</u> your child is still very important at this stage and give <u>lots of praise</u> .

4

3   LATER STILL

Your child will now be bringing home some stories s/he has not heard
before and will be wanting to tackle this unknown text on his/her own.
S/he will be using many skills learned earlier to work out the meaning.

1 How to predict or guess what is going to come next.
2 How to use the sense of the story
3 How to use the pattern of the sentence
4 How to use the pictures
5 How to use the first letter sound. All the time s/he
   will be looking   for clues to help unravel the text.

Your child may choose a book which to you may seem far too difficult.
This shows his/her confidence and enthusiasm as a reader and need not
cause you undue concern. You may be surprised at just how much of it he
can manage when it is a book he particularly wants to read.

If however s/he cannot manage any of the story to begin with just take
over the reading in the way you have done before and let the child put
in words or phrases when s/he can. Praise these efforts and keep the
reading free of anxiety.

If your child is reading most of the story with very little support
from you and just stops when s/he comes to unknown words try not to
provide the word at once.

   Instead:

      1 Wait (count to ten)
      2 Say "Try that again".Ask child to start the sentence again.
      3 Ask him/her to THINK what the word might be - what would fit the
        sense of the story.
      4 Say "Look at the picture" if this would help
      5 Say "Look at the first letter" ,this often gives a vital clue
      6 Ask the child to look at the sounds in the word.
      7 Tell the child the word.

All this is helping the child to find ways of finding out words for
him/herself.It is this which will enable children to develop
independence as a reader.
Please do not pounce on mistakes or concentrate on phonics. Phonic
rules are impossible to apply and reading in this way is full of traps

Remember that good and enthusiastic readers GUESS at words they don't
know. If the sentence doesn't make sense they have another go.
Thoughtful guessing is a valid part of the learning process and
children learn by understanding and not by blending and sounding.

5

EVENTUALLY

As your child's confidence and skill grows you will find s/he reads to you more and more. Try not to force your child to read ever increasing amounts of print. Harder books don't make better readers. The most successful readers are those who are given plenty of opportunity to read and enjoy easier books therefore gaining confidence. There is plenty of time for them to read pages of print later when confidence and a love of books have been established.

FINALLY

- Please remember that *learning to read takes time* and that children will develop at their own pace.

- Guard against competitiveness, stress and boredom.

- Foster a love of books, security and confidence.

- Most important -- KEEP IN TOUCH

Your child will be bringing her/his books home in a plastic, zip-fastening envelope. You will also find a Home-Reading Note-book containing suggestions on how to use the book chosen and how to develop your child's reading behaviour. You are welcome to write down any comments or observations.

If you have any queries please come and discuss them.

" I like the Hungry Giant because the more the words get bigger the more you have to shout "

(-Lee)

HAPPY READING

More detailed information on shared reading in school and what teachers do at each stage to ensure progress, was again offered in booklet form. Again the whole booklet (2) is illustrated.

Having looked at *why* stories, teachers at the meeting then shifted focus to *how* it all worked; *how* children learn to read using stories and *how* the teacher helps at each stage. The staff had made a video of children working in their classrooms, which showed the early stages of introducing children to the books, how the children's interest was maintained and how it was integrated into other related activities. It also showed pupils at different stages of reading development in the hope that parents might begin to recognize the natural progression of reading behaviour.

The reception class teacher was filmed using enlarged texts with the whole class. She stimulated discussion and interpretation of pictures, encouraged prediction and anticipation; used expression; pointed to the words as she read and helped the children to think about characters and situations. One boy was heard to say 'you don't find honey in dustbins' (*The Hungry Giant*, *Story Chest*, Arnold Wheaton). In the same class children were filmed in small groups listening to story tapes. They were at the stage where the text is not always matched with the spoken word and the page is often finished too quickly.

In the middle infant class individual pupils were seen using big books, headphones and tapes. Others were reading together enthusiastically, clearly able to match spoken and written words. Older infants of 6 and 7 were filmed engaged in sustained silent reading where they seemed to be making sense of the story by using a variety of different clueing systems. It was emphasized many times that although there did seem to be a pattern of reading development, individual children would progress at their own rate, according to their personality, level of maturity, experiences and opportunities.

Evaluating the success of parents' meetings

Most schools about to implement a radically new approach to reading will need to be involved at some stage in organizing large meetings of the kind described above. It is important, however, that the limitations and drawbacks of such meetings be recognized. Family and work commitments can prevent many from attending. In this respect the booklets are invaluable. Some parents may find the whole business too threatening and intimidating. Those who do attend may not feel able to voice fears or raise questions. Handled insensitively parents may feel patronized as passive recipients of 'expert' knowledge and wisdom. Meetings do not always provide opportunities for the free flow of information, ideas and opinions in both directions. They may not allow parents and teachers to plan together for the range of experiences which can promote pupil learning. Parents need to feel that they are active participants, taking an active role in real two-way partnerships. The same school described above went on to try different approaches with these principles in mind.

BOOKLET 2

AT SCHOOL

Our approach is called SHARED-READING.

How does it work ?

1 IN THE BEGINNING

The teacher will spend a lot of time sharing stories with the whole class and reading aloud from a wide range of story books.

WHY IS THIS SO IMPORTANT ?

* all children enjoy them and so want to read them for themselves;
* they get to know a lot of books and stories
* they become familiar with the language of books and stories and with the patterns and rhythms of the written word
* they learn how to read with expression
* they learn that reading is about making meaning
* they learn how BOOKS WORK :
  where they begin and end
  how to turn over the pages
  how to read from left to right
  how to enjoy the pictures

Plenty of time is allowed for talk.

WHY IS TALK SO IMPORTANT ?

* it helps children put their ideas into words
* it helps them share and explore their feelings and ideas with others
* it helps them think
* they need to look carefully at the pictures and talk about what they see
* they need to learn to tell what has happened in a story and what is going to   happen :

  Guessing what is going to come next plays a very important part in reading.
  This skill is encouraged and developed from the beginning.

  The teacher will use questions like :

  "What do you think will happen next ?"

  "What will he/she do next ?"

I

THE BOOKS

HOW ARE THEY USED ?

At this stage the books will be carefully chosen to excite the children's interest. They will have bright illustrations and may have cardboard flaps to lift to find hidden pictures and surprises.

The children will want to have these books read to them time and time again and gradually they will JOIN IN with the reading of the story.

SOON they will be so familiar with the stories they will MEMORISE them.

THIS IS AN IMPORTANT STEP TOWARDS READING

Now they will try reading them to the teacher and to other children in the class

They won't be reading the words but TELLING THE STORY

So they won't get all the words right BUT SOON they will.

It is a good way to get started.

They are acting like readers and building CONFIDENCE.

WHAT WILL THE TEACHER BE DOING TO HELP AT THIS STAGE ?

- giving ENCOURAGEMENT, PRAISE AND SUCCESS - children should never be allowed to experience failure.

- using tapes of stories and books in smaller groups

- encouraging individual children to come and 'read with me' - even if the child can only manage a few words of the text.

- allowing children to tell their own 'stories' onto tapes

- allowing them to act out/mime stories

- providing many opportunities for shared-reading ;

        as a class
        as a group
        with one partner(teacher, parent-helper, child)

      ALSO - she will be helping them learn that

          PRINT HAS MEANING

"on tape"

"Sharing a book"

HOW ?   Aaron Stua.rt

By -
*   pointing to the words as they read, making sure children recognise the left to right direction of print
*   pointing to help them match what they say with the words they see on the page
*   playing games with the words on the page
                e.g. Where does it say that ?
                    Can you find another word the same ?
*   helping them notice print all around them -
                signs, labels, letters, birthday cards
*   helping them write their names
*   encouraging them to 'play' at writing like they 'play' at reading
*   writing stories for them to read
*   writing their stories down for them
*   encouraging them to make their own books for others to read

    and
*   by reading stories to them as often as possible

3

2 LATER ON

After some time their behaviour will begin to change during story sessions.
Now they will begin to pick out words in the books and will be reading with more accuracy trying to match the spoken words with the text by pointing with a finger.

In the classroom activities will be provided which will encourage this behaviour.

WHAT ARE THEY ?

\# word games

The teacher - will miss out rhyming words for the children to complete
           - will pick out repeated words and interesting words
           - will have fun with sounds especially those to be found
             in nonsense words,'bim-bam-bumpy'/'skiddle-dee-doo'
           - will talk about first letters in words using questions
             like
           "Can you find another word that starts the same way ?"

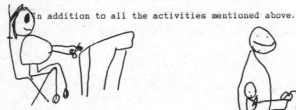

The children will be -
           - filling in missing letters and words from stories
           - copying sentences from stories
           - playing I Spy games

In addition to all the activities mentioned above.

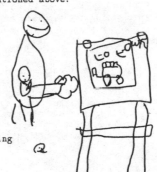

Most of all the teacher will be emphasising

READING IS THINKING and that
READING IS ABOUT MEANING.

H/She will be fostering : A LOVE OF BOOKS and providing a RELAXED,COSY ATMOSPHERE for shared- reading.

4

3 LATER STILL

Children will now be trying to read stories they have not <u>heard before.</u>
To do this they will be using:

*their store of words they recognise on sight,wordslike I,the,a,said.

* the pictures as clues

* the general sense of the story

* the first letter sound

* the pattern of the sentence

They will <u>still</u> need a great deal of support and encouragement at this
stage.

WHAT WILL THE TEACHER BE DOING TO HELP ?

S/He will be:
--praising their efforts to puzzle things out for themselves
--taking over the reading at difficult stages or if the child seems
  anxious.
--allowing mistakes - learning to read fluently requires a willingness
  to make mistakes, mistakes which the teacher will tolerate and
  accept
--giving time for child to correct the mistake by himself,using the
  sense of the story
--encouraging children to predict what the unknown words are likely to
  be by using questions like :

> "Guess what it might say ?"
> "What would make sense?"

--reading with children (still important)
--never allowing stress or boredom in reading
--giving plenty of opportunity to read and enjoy easier books and
  therefore gain <u>confidence</u>

<u>CONFIDENCE</u> is the key to success- especially at this stage

5

INDEPENDENCE IN READING

<u>When children can read on their own, how does the teacher help ?</u>

S/He will:
* keep reading stories to them
* promote their interest in books of all types
* give help in choosing books
* provide time in which to read
* give access to facts and experiences
* encourage children to imagine how others feel
* make reading easy - never forcing them to read anything too difficult to enjoy
* give training in how to use books for information using index, contents page etc.
* encourage fluent, thoughtful reading

It is most important that children must be **THINKING** readers at all levels

'Harry the Dirty Dog'

" Harry ran up stairs. They don't know he's Harry ! "
(- Erica)

Now children have achieved a fair degree of fluency the range of books they may be expected to manage will be much wider.
Picture books will still form a large part of their diet since literature plays a very important role in the growth of the imagination.

However they will be allowed to range backwards and forwards in their reading sometimes they will need undemanding, comforting books especially if something is troubling them or if they are feeling just tired.

The teacher will still be reading aloud, for this should not be limited to young children and beginning readers.
All children need to hear good stories not only for pleasure but also for emotional and mental growth.

'The Tiger who came to tea'

"The tiger drank all the water in the taps."
(-Jenny)

Now children are well on the way to becoming <u>truly literate</u>. Above all they will be reading not because they <u>HAVE</u> to but because they <u>WANT</u> to!

6

Small-group meetings

This time parents were invited personally to attend workshop type sessions of no more than 8–10 parents, plus 2 to 3 members of staff. Suggestions made in Branston and Provis (1986) for welcoming invitation cards were used. Parents sat in small groups, sometimes with a teacher sometimes without, and were invited to discuss how they felt the new approach was going, what was going well, what concerned or interested them, what they needed more help with or what they did not understand. At times it was other parents who provided the reassurance and guidance when they too had encountered similar experiences and doubts and uncertainties; a supportive, sympathetic climate is often all that some parents require. At other times, teachers led more structured discussion on specific issues like the role of phonics or record keeping or the development of writing.

Meetings of this kind do a great deal to relieve anxieties and doubts which might in the end be transferred to children. Parents develop opinions based upon experience and evidence rather than exchanging uninformed snippets of information at the school gate. This kind of fruitful partnership goes a long way towards creating 'an ethos of understanding and openness in home–school relationships' (NAHT 1988).

Other initiatives

Guidelines for home reading

These were prepared for different stages of development so that parents knew exactly what they should do and what techniques to employ (see Booklet 1 on pages 82–6). These are examples of guidelines for the very beginning stages of reading together at home.

Extract 1
Your child will be bringing home a book each day to share with you. You may find the following ideas useful as you read together.

- Look at the title and the pictures and guess what the story is about.
- Read the book with your child, following the words with your finger as you say them.
- Let your child join in when he/she can with words and sentences he/she knows.
- Allow your child to stop to talk about funny pictures or words or anything else the book reminds him/her of. You can ask questions like 'What do you think will happen next'? Guessing what comes next plays a very important part in reading.
- Let your child have the books to read and enjoy after you have shared them.

Extract 2
Your child has brought home a book bag containing a *Story Chest* book and a self-chosen library book. Please do not expect your child to be able to 'read' word

for word. Instead, I hope you will read the story *with* your child – preferably at bedtime or in a situation when he/she is feeling relaxed and comfortable. Here are a few suggestions you may find useful during your sessions together:

- Encourage your child to use the pictures to help him/her guess the text.
- Be prepared to be patient and not disappointed if he/she wants to read the same story more than once.
- Point to the words as you read them.
- Discuss the story and pictures before you turn the page. Ask the question what happens next?
- Let your child read the story to you afterwards. *Praise* all his/her attempts. Do not force participation.
- Perhaps other members of your family would like to participate in hearing your child read.
  Please note down your observations in this book.

Later on, when children began to tackle unknown texts on their own, a different set of guidelines were offered for parents to use (Figure 5.2).

As well as being of practical value, such guidance promoted confidence in teachers. Parents received advance information of clearly expressed aims and objectives and regular reassurance on issues which are known to cause misunderstanding and concern (e.g. phonics). Above all, parents began to understand what was expected of them!

Home-reading notebooks

As home–school partnerships developed at this school some teachers sought to involve parents in planning more reading experiences at home, in analysing children's behaviour with text, in assessing and recording progress. Much of this was achieved through the use of a home-reading notebook in which parents were invited to make comments and observations on significant reading behaviours and responses.

The dialogue between Jenny's parents and her teacher, serves to illustrate the value of open, trusting home–school partnerships. While undoubtedly time consuming, it can become for all concerned one of the most rewarding aspects of a real-book, shared-reading approach.

Jenny's story

Jenny's parents were very sceptical about the new story-based approach. Their two elder children had learnt to read using reading schemes and they saw no need for change. Jenny's mother wrote much later,

> I felt very negative about the whole thing. It seemed too 'experimental' and revolutionary and also I was worried about change for change's sake. I couldn't imagine how Jenny was *ever* going to learn to read with this seemingly casual approach.

What made the situation worse was that Jenny, like Kevin, was slow to develop concepts of print and to move from one stage to the next. Although she had benefited from the experiences of a literate home, Jenny was just a little slow in getting started and needed time to mature.

Your child will now be bringing home some stories he/she has not heard before and will be wanting to tackle this unknown text on his/her own. He/she will be using many of the skills learnt in the beginning stages to work out the meaning:

- How to predict or 'guess' what is going to come next.
- How to use the sense of the story.
- How to use the pattern of the sentence.
- How to use the pictures.
- How to use the first letter sound.

In addition he/she will have built up a store of words that he can recognize on sight.

Your child may choose a book which to you may seem far too difficult. Do not worry about this. It shows his/her confidence and his/her enthusiasm as a reader! You may be surprised at just how much of it he/she can manage when it is a book he/she particularly wants to read.

If, however, he/she cannot manage any of the story to begin with just take over the reading for him/her in the way you have done before and let him/her put in words or phrases when he/she can. Praise his/her efforts and keep the reading free of anxiety. Enjoy the story together.

If your child is reading most of the story with very little support from you and just stops when he/she comes to unknown words, here are a few suggestions for you to try:

- Count to ten. This will give child a chance to think and work it out for him/herself.
- Say **try that again**. Ask child to start the sentence again.
- Ask him/her to **think** what the word might be, using the sense of the story.
- Say **look at the picture** if that could help.
- Say **look at the first letter** – this often gives a vital clue.
- Ask him/her to look at the **sounds** in the word.
- **Tell** him/her the word.

All this is helping the child to find ways of figuring out words for him/herself. It is this which will enable him/her to develop independence as a reader.

Please do not pounce on mistakes or concentrate on phonics. Phonic rules are impossible to apply and reading in this way is full of traps.

Remember that good and enthusiastic readers **guess** at words they don't know. If the sentence doesn't make sense they have another go. Thoughtful guessing is a valid part of the learning process and children learn by understanding and not by blending and sounding.

Above all enjoy reading.
Praise and smile!
Books are fun!

Figure 5.2 Guidelines for parents helping children to read unknown texts

With frequent shared reading of familiar self-chosen texts, Jenny's responses gradually began to mature and she started to display the kinds of reading behaviour indicative of a growing awareness of the different functions and features of written language. Significantly, Jenny's parents were the first to recognize this growth in insight and as we see below, used the home-reading notebook to express undoubted relief and delight:

> Jenny picked out 'go', quite unasked, from her bedtime books, I was thrilled! This is the first time she's done anything like that. She also noticed that some have big 'G' and some little 'g'.
>
> Thank you again for taking so much trouble to reassure me over the reading scheme. I feel so much happier about it now. Thanks again.

The partnership that existed between the parent and the teacher prevented anxiety from being projected on to the beginning reader. Jenny never doubted that reading was fun and worthwhile. She believed in herself as a reader and responded to stories in a wonderful way as this extract shows:

> Jenny read us *The Ghost* over and over again, and read it to every visitor and each of her dolls! I think she really likes it! We enjoyed reading some of Mog.

The notebooks were also used to keep parents informed as to what was happening at school and what the teacher was doing to help. In this way they provided on-going dialogue between school and home. Jenny was encouraged to create her own reading material to share with her school friends and parents:

> Jenny is writing her own 'book' about her holiday. Children often learn to read using their own self-made books. The stories they create themselves have, of course, great power and meaning and usually never fail to be read back weeks, months later. She will be thrilled when it is finally ready to be brought home!

Jenny was also invited to bring 'work' done at home into school. These highly personal efforts were often woven into school literacy events like book making or illustrated display work.

The entries in the notebook helped the teacher to build a detailed profile of Jenny as a reader both at home and at school. The reference to *Alfie* (Shirley Hughes) and the blanket shows how the sharing of stories in this home was very much an integral part of everyday family happenings and routines and how Jenny was able to make links between what she found in books and her own real-life experiences. This and the *Lazy Mary* extract are also interesting from the point of view that here we see a parent beginning to accept that reading is a complex act, involving the combination of a variety of different clueing strategies like the ability to use context to self-correct and reread when text fails to make sense. It is no longer a simple process of 'getting words right'. We can also see how the parent is beginning to use a kind of 'meta-language' to describe the reading process: 'She is still not always achieving a 1/1 match' and 'going back to correct herself using the pictures'. This was a direct outcome of frequent open dialogue between home and school. With a real-book approach this shared common understanding of both process and terminology is particularly important.

> Jenny read to N.Y. perfectly, even going back to correct herself, using the pictures. This made her feel good, I think. We enjoyed *Alfie* especially as we too have a bit of blanket, affectionately called 'nigh-nigh'! We made great fun out of that.

> We did *Lazy Mary* anyway. As you say, she is still not always achieving a 1/1 match. Your suggestion of word games worked out well and seemed to help.

> The enclosed picture is an example of the kind of thing she does at home, I'm so glad this is what you want her to do. It's difficult sometimes to know if these are along the right lines or if I should be gently guiding her to do something else, so this communication between you and I is very valuable from this respect.

The effectiveness of such dialogues depended on the existence of an ethos based on respect, understanding and openness. Such a shared commitment of honesty and trust enabled both parent and teacher to share the moments of fun and happiness as well as those of concern and doubt, as we see by these extracts:

> I do sometimes wonder about this new approach to reading; having already helped two older children to learn to read, this method seems to me to be very 'hit and miss'. I do, nevertheless, make it enjoyable for Jenny. We're all very keen on reading in our family and 'reading' aloud is nothing new to Jenny. (I hope these comments don't seem negative to you, they're *not* intended to be!)

> Thank you again for all your patience and the interest you so freely show in the children. I would like to go to the meeting that you've mentioned. I'm sure it would be time really well spent, and would give *me* the encouragement I sometimes need! Jenny is enjoying her reading again now after going through a very 'anti' stage. It's such a relief to see how after this 'sticky time' I can *see* progress now which is so encouraging for me!

Jenny did break through to each stage in her own time and at her own pace. Undoubtedly her parents were concerned about her apparent lack of 'measurable' progress, but the close relationship established with the teacher provided support and endless reassurance. Jenny was never allowed to feel a failure and gradually began to move towards more and more independence in reading.

> Jenny read both of these with great confidence and enjoyment. Patience is indeed being rewarded! I've spent quite a bit of time recently reassuring friends that children do indeed learn to read with *Story Chest!*

So the teacher gained a new ambassador!

This particular home–school initiative embodied many of the same principles and forms of assessment now recommended by the Report of the *Task Group on Assessment and Testing* (DES 1988b). It was essentially 'formative' in that information on the child's attainment was used to help both parent and teacher plan for the next stages. In this it offered both 'feedback' and 'feed-forward'. It was spontaneous and continuous and rather than being simply 'bolted on at the end'; it was integral to the learning process.

It was part of ordinary family reading activities – as the parents shared stories with their child they were also carefully observing and assessing attitudes and responses to books and behaviour with texts. They did not use 'out of context' texts, like checking words known on reading cards or in lists at the back of books. It also involved parents in diagnosing specific reading behaviour, as we saw earlier in extracts from the reading notebook.

All this information, together with that collected on the same basis by the teacher in the classroom, contributed towards a very detailed profile of individual progress and achievement. This mass of information needed collating at regular intervals so that it could be made more accessible to other interested parties like the headteacher and other members of staff. Three examples of such a profile are shown in (Figures 5.3, 5.4, 5.5).

Many parents used the home-reading notebook to maintain similarly close dialogues with the teachers. They found them a reassuring way of 'keeping in touch' when work and family commitments prevented them from seeing the teacher regularly. Some entries simply recorded the date and books shared, with perhaps a few brief comments, especially if all was well.

However, a few parents could not or did not wish to respond in this way. The teachers then tried to keep lines of communication open by inviting parents to come into school to help their child choose a book at the end of the day. If this was not possible, older brothers and sisters were encouraged to share books with younger siblings. Unfortunately, despite every effort there will be some, who for one reason or another, simply do not receive the parental support and encouragement they need. For such children the involvement of other parents within schools and classrooms can be particularly important.

Parental help in classrooms

A small group of parent helpers was able to work alongside teachers on a regular basis, supporting and extending the wide range of literacy activities on offer. Sometimes they would read stories aloud to individual pupils or small groups of three or four. At other times they would be situated in the book corner and available to share a book. They also helped children to create their own reading material using the many different kinds of book making possible (see page 49).

When parents enter into such classroom partnerships with teachers more children obviously have more opportunities to engage in meaningful literacy events with adults. However, it is vital that certain children are not made to feel that they are in some way 'weaker' or less successful readers than their peers. A strong, positive self-image as a reader is crucial to success with a real-book approach. The pervading philosophy should always be that some pupils may be simply more 'experienced' than others.

ATTITUDE/RESPONSE

Laura enjoys listening to stories and will share books with adults and friends but she does not often freely choose during the day. She does lack a little self-confidence and is rather quiet, sometimes needing encouragement to relate her thoughts and experiences to adults.

Nevertheless, she has favourites and she is developing more confidence with these.

POSSIBLE TEACHER INTERVENTION

- Provide support through praise and encouragement to increase confidence.
- Encourage talk about her own experiences.

BEHAVIOUR WITH TEXT

Mainly shared-reading with adult. Will finger-point, sliding finger under text. Watches print and pictures.

Beginning to attempt favourites alone. Retelling becoming more accurate each time but still sliding finger under the print.

Uses memory and pictures to retell stories.

- Lots of shared reading to increase confidence. (With other children in pairs/groups, older children, other adults.)
- Use tapes and big books to develop familiarity with books.
- Encourage anticipation and prediction skills in retelling stories.

WHAT HE/SHE KNOWS

How a book works:
  the cover,
  to start on the left,
  direction l–r
  top–bottom
Can interpret pictures
Can use pictures to retell and sequence simple familiar stories.
Understanding of stories is somewhat limited.
Recognizes her name.
Aware of print.
Aware text tells story.
Understanding of rhyme is limited.

- Lots of rhymes to develop understanding of rhyme. Play rhyming games → anticipation of rhymes.
- Encourage her to talk more about stories and why things happen.
- Develop awareness of print in environment.
- Develop retelling and sequencing stories by using tapes/puppets.

Figure 5.3 Primary school reading profile – Laura

ATTITUDE/RESPONSE

Donna is a bookworm and loves listening to stories. She especially likes to share a wide variety of stories with her friends, and is always willing to read her favourites to adults.

She is now beginning to widen her selection of books to include storybooks other than solely *Story Chest* – a sign that her confidence continues to grow. She gets very involved in the stories and is beginning to use her voice quite well.

BEHAVIOUR WITH TEXT

With familiar texts. Reads accurately with l–l word–sound match.

Uses phonics, contexts and pictures to help tackle unknown texts and words with adult support.

Self-corrects when makes mistakes.

Is slowly beginning to attempt unfamiliar texts.

WHAT HE/SHE KNOWS

Aware of cover of book and title.

Developing a vague awareness of author.

Knows where to start reading, which direction to take, how to turn pages.

Has very good understanding of stories.

Is able to use pictures to tell and sequence stories.

Has good powers of prediction and anticipation with familiar stories.

Is beginning to discuss why events happen.

Aware of text. Matches word–sound.

Understands print carries a message.

Very extensive sight vocabulary.

Beginning to develop phonic awareness. Uses initial sounds to attack unfamiliar words.

Can use a word-book.

Recognises names.

Can use an index/contents page and find page.

Understands concepts of words, letters. Aware of full stops.

POSSIBLE TEACHER INTERVENTION

- Promote confidence to tackle more unknown texts by providing as much support as she likes. Use library as a resource.
- Use her enjoyment of books to help other children in paired/group sessions.
- Encourage increased awareness of reference books.

- Needs positive support to maintain confidence. Encourage her to scan ahead, use anticipation and prediction skills, use sounds in a word when tackling known and unfamiliar texts.
- Encourage her to use the skills she has developed already – using sight vocabulary, pictures etc.

- Develop study skills by using more anthologies, continuing use of word-book.
- Promote existing skills by encouraging use of books for information in other curriculum areas.
- Draw more attention to punctuation.
- Focus on sounds and words through written work.

Figure 5.4 Primary school reading profile – Donna

ATTITUDE/RESPONSE	POSSIBLE TEACHER INTERVENTION
David is a most enthusiastic reader. Appreciates a wide variety of material from nonsense rhymes, plays, through to non-fiction. Books on 'technical' subjects and his current favourites. Enjoys sharing books with peers and his conversations show a mature, perceptive level of thought. Book-reviews are showing signs of developing critical skills.	Provide a supply of non-fiction at the right readability level to promote this interest and develop project work.
BEHAVIOUR WITH TEXT	
A thinking reader – frequently self-corrects. Concentrates very hard on the general sense of the story. Needs to be encouraged to work out unknown words for himself at times (waiting for 10 seconds – v. effective as he puzzles out.) Makes good use of contextual cues – will often carry on with the rest of the sentence and back-track to unknown word. Interpretation of pictures well developed and being put to use with books like: 'Things that go'. Reads with expression and obvious enjoyment.	David would benefit from some phonic practice – as it arises and as appropriate.
WHAT HE/SHE KNOWS	
Story and print concepts very well developed. Study skills impressive for C Age. David is using a dictionary and can find information project work, although copies verbatim at present. Family visit library regularly. Beginning to extract information from factual books + reading to *learn* Teacher: C. Burman Date 26.6	David is more than ready for this type of work! He will *need* help in reporting/re-drafting information for topic work.

Figure 5.5   Primary school reading profile – David

Conclusions

This chapter has discussed home–school partnerships, especially in the beginning stages of reading. It has explored some of the ways parents can become active participants in supporting their children's development as readers by describing how one school involved parents in various kinds of partnerships.

Jenny's parents are typical of those who became deeply involved and their home-reading notebook is a powerful, sometimes moving account of their embracing a real reading approach which at first seemed too 'experimental' and 'revolutionary'. It stands to reassure all concerned that parents *can* develop a more sophisticated view of the complex reading process and achievement if and when the teachers take the time to explain what they are doing and why they are doing it.

Not every school would wish to adopt exactly the kinds of partnerships detailed in this chapter. Different schools will need to identify different ways of involving different sets of parents depending upon need and local factors. What is important is that in some way parents have *opportunities* to develop positive and supportive partnerships with schools. When this happens everyone can benefit. These parental comments after two years of a real-book approach, clearly show this to be the case, and it is appropriate to leave parents with the last words . . .

I can see my own children paying much more attention to books than I did at that age. Books to me were boring but I didn't have Spot or Meg and Mog I had to find out for myself that books were interesting and that was just by chance. At least we are giving children the chance to find out about books and that they are not just for learning but for enjoyment. I think we are giving them the best start with this scheme and that they will continue to read for enjoyment and pleasure in the future.

In answer to your questions on opposite page, my feelings about the reading scheme when it started were very mixed. When you have been used to doing things a certain way for many years and have taught one child to read on the old scheme you wonder why there has to be change, after all millions of children did learn to read on the old scheme and I wondered if the new reading scheme was bought in just for the sake of change. So I was very sceptical about it all. I now feel my scepticism was due to ignorance about the new reading scheme. It has taken some time for me to understand the scheme and at times was ready to give up on it all but perseverance by teachers in explaining things has finally started to pay off. I think if you take the time to understand the scheme you can see the benefits to children. Parents can take a greater part in helping their child to learn. Think the more talks and meetings we have for parents about this scheme the better for parents to be informed.

I would just like to say that when the reading scheme first started, I thought it would confuse all the young children who had just got used to the system of flash cards and word cards that were kept in a tin. But this new scheme is better because children don't feel left out, they can have a go at reading any book on display. They don't feel that they have to read a whole set before moving on to a new set. There is no contest to win.

Freddie started on the reading chest after two terms at his previous school where the 'Through the Rainbow' scheme was used. Previously, what he read at school bore no resemblance to his interest in books at home.

Although he did not use *Story Chest* books for very long, I think the philosophy of interest in reading, as applied to the other books he chose, contributed greatly to his rapid progress in reading. He has always been keen to read, but this has been reinforced by your attitude at school.

We, as parents, particularly enjoyed the exchange of views with the teacher through the book of comments on home reading; I think it might be quite useful to continue this on an occasional basis (we appreciate the effort it takes for busy teachers) even at this higher level of reading.

I feel that you are doing a lot to help the children to read by this new reading programme, but I think it is not just the children who must want to read, but also the parents must be encouraged to keep the children's interest in books going both in school and just as important at home. Because without the parents' support with home reading, use of the local library, etc. there is a danger that books are only associated by the children with school and weekdays and not something to be enjoyed at weekends and holiday time.

At first when I heard about the *Story Chest* I was rather apprehensive about how the story-based approach could be as successful as the traditional methods used to teach children to read. I felt reluctant to accept a change from traditional methods of teaching, but have to admit now that any fears I had were totally unfounded, because the new scheme is a huge success. I am really very impressed with the way the children have learnt very quickly and really enjoy reading.

David has progressed really well, and can tackle books which I thought would be too difficult for him. He reads anything in sight, newspapers, notice boards, adverts etc.

Yes, he really enjoys books of all types and of varying degrees of difficulty. Sometimes he chooses 'simple' books and sometimes very 'adult' books. He enjoys factual and fictional books.

I haven't noticed any difference in attitude with older children. The only problem has been to accept change and to re-educate myself to a totally different technique of reading.

Claire had started to learn to read before coming to *Story Chest* but she took to the books instantly and liked the idea of being able to 'read' a book immediately, although at first she was only remembering the story after it had been read to her. She has been using this approach for almost a year now and I feel she has progressed very well. Going quickly from remembering the story to recognising words and then reading properly.

6 Resources for teaching

BARRIE WADE

This chapter is organized in two sections to provide further resources for teaching and learning. Section A (Working with story) is essentially a practical guide to key features of an effective classroom programme. It is not exhaustive and teachers will need to supplement it with their own knowledge about the particular children they teach.

Section B is likewise practical and specific, being organized as annotated booklists. I have deliberately made these lists selective and again they will need supplementing by individual parents and teachers. They are meant to provide starting points for future expansion or to supplement existing practice. They are, of course, not meant to be worked through slavishly or to represent *all* that is valuable in children's literature.

A. Working with story

Partnership with parents

Encourage parents to take a positive role in story and reading from the beginning. The parent you think is unconcerned may really be reluctant to interfere. With your encouragement to parents children can progress dramatically. Remember parents usually have much more opportunity to create a one-to-one learning environment than you do. Try

- Running a story and reading workshop for parents.
- Encouraging some parents to help regularly in your classroom.
- To become an informed source of information on children's books.
- Giving parents a leaflet like those in Chapter 5.

Parents are glad to have your professional advice, so give it confidently. For example, encourage them to:

- Take children to the library regularly.
- Make reading *fun* and read only interesting books.

- Read aloud to children regularly.
- Listen to children's stories and tell their own. Share jokes and rhymes.
- Talk about stories with children.
- Let children see that *they* enjoy reading.
- Praise their children's interest and achievement.

and two practical essentials that might be forgotten:

- Fix a bookshelf in the child's bedroom.
- Fix a reading light so that the child can read in bed.

The classroom book collection

Begged, bought or borrowed – it makes little difference since the end justifies the means!

- Add to class resources by bringing in your own books.
- Encourage children to bring theirs.
- Gifts from parents and loans from library services are useful supplements.
- Run a bookshop for pupils and parents from the classroom.
- Run a purchasing book club which will provide some free copies for your shelves as well as books for children to own.

A rich variety of books

Aim to provide books for all moods – some to extend and challenge, some to skim through, some to offer just relaxation. As well as having a wide range of authors, have a rich variety of kinds of books: funny, sad, fictional, biographical, practical, fantastic, realistic, expository, reflective and lots of verse. On the same shelves have books written by children in your class as well as published collections by children, e.g. *Children as Writers* (Heinemann). Have books of folk tales and myths from other lands and books about other cultures. Read reviews of children's books in, for example, the *Times Educational Supplement* and *The School Librarian* for new ideas.

Tolerance, identification and understanding of a rich diversity of stories are important positive outcomes of using stories in other cultures. All children enjoy:

- folk tales, myths and legends from many lands.
- stories set in other times and cultures.
- listening to stories in their first language.
- listening to taped stories in English.
- retelling legends and traditional stories.

Try

- taping stories in English so children can read and listen.
- encouraging parents to tell stories in *both* first language and English.
- encouraging older brothers and sisters to do the same.

- making dual text story books:
  - obtain written translations from someone in the community.
  - insert these on cards or (more successfully) on strips stuck under or above the English text.
  - obtain taped readings of the story translations.

Where reading thrives

Make the whole classroom a place where reading thrives by having lots of books on display, encouraging their use and promoting a quiet atmosphere.

- Maybe turn one area into a specially inviting reading corner with a carpet or floor cushions and even an armchair.
- Use this corner for book displays and some story-telling sessions.
- Always present books attractively.
- Occasionally make a feature display on a theme.
- Check shelving heights are easily accessible to children.

Read yourself!

Enjoy your own stories, let children see your satisfaction and share it with them. Keep a book you are enjoying on your desk and let children see you reading it occasionally. Children are not fools and it is surprising how often what we recommend fails to take root because we do not do it ourselves.

Some schools have successfully experimented with USSR (not a subversive activity, but Uninterrupted Sustained Silent Reading). At a specific time in the week everyone in the whole school stops what they are doing and picks up a book for about 20 quiet minutes. 'Everyone' means just that, including headteacher, secretary, caretaker and any parents or advisers who may be there at the time!

- Enthuse about books and the pleasure they give you.
- Talk about books you have read.
- Be honest about those you did not enjoy.

Make time for reading

Sharing books together is a focal point of whole class activities.

- Read aloud frequently and, if enough texts are not available, occasionally put short passages on an overhead projector for all to follow.
- Give time throughout the week for browsing through the class library and maybe use the books there to develop individualized reading.
- Do not be afraid to let children take books home from the very beginning of reading. That is where most sustained reading will be done.

On the other hand also make regular time (perhaps as an optional activity) for this kind of extended reading in school. We do not normally read books only in five minute bursts.

Pleasure not pressure

Very young school children can distinguish between 'real' books and 'reading' books. Some reading schemes used in classrooms say to children 'reading is boring' because their books are boring. Check that your schemes are based upon

- the language people use in real life.
- forward-moving, coherent narratives.
- stories that give pleasure in themselves.

If they are not, seek to change them.

No amount of pressure to complete (or compete to finish) a scheme can make up for a lack of pleasure in reading. We are in the business of creating readers for a lifetime not forcing children to jump through the hoops of a graded scheme for their own sake.

- Start with the expectation that reading is fun.
- Give children a chance to talk about their pleasure.
- Let a child change a book that has become boring or stale.

Hands on

One infant school which is experimenting with computer programmes in the teaching of reading encourages 'hands on' experience of computer keyboards by children from their first days at school. Curiously the same school refuses to allow children to take home library books until they have completed both the computer programmes and the last book of a graded series of reading primers. Yet children need the experience of handling a variety of books whose sequencing, double-page arrangement and simultaneous mix of illustration and text are not the same as part-page computer displays. Give plenty of hands-on experience with real books from the beginning. It is a necessary part of what reading is. There are many children who are only motivated to progress in reading through their interests in dinosaurs or aeroplanes that are fostered by library books.

- Let children take books home.
- Encourage borrowing from public libraries.
- Encourage purchase of books.

Polish your own skills

Celebrate story by re-creating moods and feelings as well as the ideas behind words on the printed page. Work on your skills as a story teller and story reader.

Story telling

- Pick a story you really enjoy.
- Try it out a few times (in front of a mirror can help).

- Use all your resources (movement, voice, gesture, facial expression).
- Involve the children (joining in repetitions and choruses, guessing what will happen).
- Use aids, puppets or illustrations (try simple sketches on the blackboard or overhead projector as you go).

Story reading

An expressive, fluent reading by the teacher is the best way to help children re-create a story's meaning. Some hints:

- Know the story well (so that you can dramatize it effectively).
- Try out a reading to get the feelings right.
- Experiment with different voices for different characters.
- Check all children are sitting so that they can see you (your expressions and eye contact can be important) and if necessary the illustrations (a compact group is better than isolated children in rows).
- Do not interrupt your story by asking questions. When you have finished, they will come from the children.

Use other media

Schools broadcasts on both radio and television have excellent story tellings and dramatizations which can be recorded, stored in class and played back by individuals (perhaps using headphones) or groups. A good deal of commercially produced material on tape is also available.

- Try encouraging children to make their own tapes.
- Make a story from a newspaper headline or summary.
- Make a tape/slide story.

Children act out any suitable story, say *Rosie's Walk, Where the Wild Things Are* or *The Shrinking of Treehorn*. Make slides of their version. Then record children narrating the story and put the slides and tape together to make a permanent (and popular) programme. The video camera is an excellent alternative.

Follow-up activities

Sometimes it is best to have no systematic follow up. After all, enjoyment of literature is the main aim and we do not want to overkill. Remember the boy who saw the rabbit on a nature walk, 'Quick,' said his friend, 'look the other way or Miss'll make us write about it'.

Children can:

- Tell each other about similar experiences in their own lives.
- Write a sequel.
- Talk in small groups (without an adult) about the story and the people in it.
- Design a paperback cover.

- Retell the story perhaps from one character's view.
- Make a radio drama of a scene.
- Act out a scene.
- Write about their feelings as they read or listen.
- Illustrate the story in pictures round the walls.
- Make puppet characters and use them to enact the story.

Encourage story telling by children

Oral stories are an important part of our culture and literature.
Encourage a relaxed atmosphere for:

- exchange of anecdotes, jokes, yarns, experiences.
- retelling of well-known stories.
- invention of new stories.
- children in groups to take it in turns to tell part of a story.

Make sure *you* listen attentively and that the children know you do.

Rhymes and rhythm

Use plenty of nursery and playground rhymes. They are fun. They work through repetition and the patterns of rhythm and sound. They are frequently stories in themselves.

- Use them on overhead projectors as alternatives to reading primers.
- Speak them aloud.
- Do the actions.
- Mime the expressions and feelings.
- Make up more rhymes and verses together.
- Read lots of poetry aloud.
- Work together on class poems.

Children as writers

Let children write their own stories from the early years. They have plenty of experience of what story is from their own games, anecdotes and stories they have heard.

- Have a special book for stories or have loose leaves pinned together in an illustrated cover.
- Tape-record or write down yourself the spoken stories of children who have severe difficulty with the mechanics of writing.
- Encourage children to revise their drafts.
- Sometimes allow children to revise each other's drafts.
- Encourage small groups to work on writing collaboratively.
- Make up stories as a whole class.

- Encourage individual and collaborative book-making (narrative or non-narrative) for real audiences.

Stories into plays

Well-known stories that have been read in class are good starting points. Books, poems, stories from TV, parents and actual experience are other sources. Try different techniques:

- Improvise entirely.
- Use a narrator and characters to improvise.
- Groups prepare a script, redraft, try out and revise.

Share with children what they read

What matters essentially is that children do read and are entertained by reading. They are more likely to take recommendations from you if you share (and do not disapprove of) what *they* read.

- Talk about comics and TV programmes.
- Share jokes, songs.
- Listen to stories of their experiences and retellings of what they have read.

Encourage genuine response

If you treat poems and stories as exercises in comprehension you cannot complain if children behave as if they were being *tested*. They are! It is doubtful whether literature can be taught. Certainly there is no point in testing before children have learned to respond. Help children to re-create for themselves the meanings of stories and poems.

Powerful response may come indirectly. Watch for it in:

- making posters and book covers.
- keeping a reader's diary.
- writing a related poem or story.
- painting a picture.
- spontaneous talk.
- rereading the book.
- retelling the story.
- dramatizing a scene or story incident.
- going on to another book.

Watch and listen

- Listen to children's everyday anecdotes.
- Listen to children retelling stories they have read.
- Listen to children talking about books.
- Watch for a breakthrough: the book that stirs interest, develops understanding in groups or individuals.

- Watch what children do as they engage with story.
- Watch for the child who stops reading with interest.
- Watch a child reading a story and see what strategies are used.

B. Booklists

The booklists that follow in this section are meant to provide starting points for children, teachers and parents. They do not claim to be exhaustive. They are, as they are described, select booklists. I have not provided lists of all the books by particular authors, for example, and I have often omitted excellent material which I assume, because of its popularity, to be well known. The lists are select because they also depend upon the preference of the compiler! I have been fortunate, however, in making my choice (and in revising the original selections) to be able to draw upon the knowledge and experience of Judith Elkin, ex-Children's Librarian for the City of Birmingham and Lecturer in Library Studies at the Birmingham Polytechnic. I am grateful to her for this help and to share the responsibility of choice with her.

The lists give a brief review account of what is to be found in the book. These annotations are necessarily brief but I believe they will make the list more valuable than the bare bones of those which simply give title, author and publisher. I have attempted to give guidance for the age range of children for whom particular books are suitable. I must emphasize that these are guidelines and may need to be modified in the light of experience with particular children.

Finally, the list is organized into separate sections:

- picture books
- pop-up books
- collections of stories, tales and poems
- poetry
- fiction
- information books written in story form

Select list of books
Picture books

Lend Me Your Wings	John Agard, Hodder A charming crick-crack story in which Sister Fish and Brother Bird swap places for the day. 5–8
The Jolly Postman	Janet and Allan Ahlberg, Heinemann The jolly postman delivers letters to various familiar folk-tale characters: each letter comes in its own envelope. A simple idea, developed visually and imaginatively, ideal for sharing and exploring. 3–13
Burglar Bill	Janet and Allan Ahlberg, Picture Lion The lovable Burglar Bill mends his ways when confronted with Burglar Betty. 5–8

Mishka	Victor Ambrus, Oxford University Press
	Mishka seeks fame in a circus. 5–8
The Lighthouse Keeper's Lunch	Ronda and David Armitage, Puffin/Deutsch
	How can the lighthouse keeper keep the seagulls off his sandwiches? 5–8
Patrick	Quentin Blake, Puffin/Cape
	The magic of music transforms the world. 3–8
Mister Magnolia	Quentin Blake, Cape Picture Lion
	Colourful, zany illustrations and enchanting simple rhythm make Mister Magnolia who has 'only one boot' a great favourite. 3–8
Through My Window	Tony Bradman, Methuen
	Jo stays away from school for a day and watches through the window. As she waits anxiously for her mother to come home, she sees a succession of non-stereotyped characters (female window cleaner, etc.). 3–7
My Brother Sean	Petronella Breinberg, illustrated by Errol Lloyd, Picture Puffin
	Sean goes to nursery school and cries! A familiar, warm story about a small black child. See also *Doctor Sean* and *Sean's Red Bike*. 3–8
Father Christmas	Raymond Briggs, Hamish Hamilton/Puffin
	Cartoon strip illustrations provide an irreverent but none the less appealing portrait of Father Christmas on his rounds. In *Father Christmas Goes on Holiday* we see him relaxing, although still somewhat grumpy. 5–11
The Snowman	Raymond Briggs, Puffin/Hamish Hamilton
	A splendid picture sequence of a boy's exciting (and moving) adventure with his snowman friend. 3–8
Piggybook	Anthony Browne, Julia MacRae Books
	Mr Piggott and his two sons are waited on hand and foot by Mrs Piggott, until finally she leaves them to their own devices. Gradually everything (themselves, the wallpaper, the doorknobs) take on the shape of pigs: a charming poke at stereotypes. 5–13
Willy the Wimp	Anthony Browne, Julia MacRae Books
	Willy, determined to overcome his nickname the Wimp, takes up bodybuilding but discovers that drastic changes are difficult. Simple text, humorous illustrations. Try also *Willy the Champ*. 5–9
Come Away from the Water, Shirley	John Burningham, Cape
	Imaginative and actual experiences are presented for comparison. The result is a very funny book. See also *Time to Get out of the Bath, Shirley*. 5–9
Grandpa	John Burningham, Cape
	A perceptive visual story of the close relationship between a grandfather and his granddaughter, which ends with the poignant emptiness of his chair signifying his death. 5–9

Mr Gumpy's Outing	John Burningham, Picture Puffin
	A lovely story told with effective repetition of a special boat ride. **3–8**
The Cat Who Thought He Was a Tiger	Polly Cameron, Picture Puffin/Deutsch
	What imagination can do for an ordinary cat until he goes to a circus and meets the real thing. **3–8**
Dear Zoo	Rod Campbell, Abelard
	A book written like a letter with the chance for readers to make guesses as they go on. **3–8**
The Very Hungry Caterpillar	Eric Carle, Picture Puffin/Hamish Hamilton
	Caterpillars will eat just about anything. Even books are not safe. **3–8**
The Trouble With Mum	Babette Cole, Kaye and Ward
	Why don't other parents get on with mum? It's not just the hats she wears. Maybe it's because she rides a broomstick. **3–8**
Fourteen Rats and a ratcatcher	James Cressey, Black/Puffin
	The little old lady would be very happy if it weren't for the 14 nasty rats living under her floor; similarly, the 14 rats would be very happy if it weren't for the nasty little old lady! **3–8**
Jungle Jumble	Robert Crowther, Kestrel
	Children have fun making their own stories from the juxtapositions of pictures. **3–8**
Hairy Maclary from Donaldson's Dairy	Lynley Dodd, Spindlewood
	An amusing, cumulative rhyme about Hairy Maclary and his friends: 'Bottomley Potts all covered in spots; Hercules Morse as big as a horse'. **3–8**
The Patchwork Quilt	Valerie Flournoy, Bodley Head
	Grandma is old and making a patchwork quilt for her granddaughter is her way of weaving together the strands of the family's past. An evocative story. **7–9**
Moose	Michael Foreman, Picture Puffin/Hamish Hamilton
	What does peace-loving Moose do when noisy creatures start throwing things around? **3–8**
Shrewbettina's Birthday	John Goodall, Macmillan
	Shrewbettina's party and the preparations for it are cleverly narrated in pictures. **3–8**
Teddybears 1 to 10 *Teddybear's ABC*	Suzanna Gretz, Ernest Benn/Puffin
	Delightfully mischievous and individual teddies in all sorts of peculiar scrapes; for slightly older children *The Teddybear's Moving Day* **3–8**
Roger Takes Charge!	Suzanna Gretz, Bodley Head
	Roger decides to take charge when Flo from next door gets too bossy. Delightful domestic scenes of these popular pigs. See also *It's Your Turn, Roger!* **5–9**
Crafty Chameleon	Mwenye Hadithi, Hodder
	Chameleon finally outwits the cunning leopard and crocodile in this brilliant colourful traditional tale from Kenya. **5–7**

Maybe It's a Tiger	Kathleen Hersom, Macmillan Papermac
	Children engage in fantasy play about a zoo, gathering the nearest animals they can find to the pictures in little Joseph's book. 3–8
Best Friends for Frances	Russel Hoban, illustrated Lilian Hoban, Faber
	What it's like to be left out of the fun. Try also *Bedtime for Frances*. 3–8
Alfie Gets in First	Shirley Hughes, Bodley Head
	Alfie locks Mum and baby sister outside. A familiar situation for small children and a splendid talking point. See also *Alfie's Feet, Alfie Lends a Hand* and *An Evening at Alfie's*. 3–8
Dogger	Shirley Hughes, Bodley Head/Picture Lion
	Dave is inconsolable when he loses his favourite toy and constant companion, Dogger. Another splendid portrait of a familiar crisis. 3–8
1 Hunter	Pat Hutchins, Picture Puffin/Bodley Head
	A brilliantly funny narrative with pictures and text in counterpoint. 3–8
Rosie's Walk	Pat Hutchins, Picture Puffin/Bodley Head
	Rosie the hen goes her own sweet way with not a care for the dangers behind. 3–8
Don't Forget the Bacon	Pat Hutchins, Picture Puffin/Bodley Head
	What a mix up in the shopping list! Repetition, anticipation, it's all here! 3–8
Hi, Cat!	Ezra Jack Keats, Picture Puffin/Bodley Head
	Archie's greeting to the black cat is only the start of his problem. 3–8
Whistle for Willie *The Snowy Day*	Ezra Jack Keats, Bodley Head/Puffin
	A small boy learning and experiencing new things around him. 3–8
Peter's Chair *Through the Window*	Charles Keeping, Oxford University Press
	Jacob, fed up and alone, watches events in the street outside his house 'through the window'. 5–11
The Tiger Who Came to Tea	Judith Kerr, Collins
	You would expect a tiger to be greedy, wouldn't you? 3–8
Jafta	Hugh Lewin, Evans/Dinosaur
	Jafta, a young African boy talks about his family in simple prose. Delightful illustrations. See also *Jafta – My Mother, Jafta – My Father*. 3–8
Not Now, Bernard	David McKee, Andersen Press/Sparrow Books
	Every child will sympathize with Bernard whose parents are too busy to listen, even when he says a monster is going to eat him up . . . it does! 3–8
Flossie and the Fox	Patricia McKissack, Kestrel
	Smart Flossie outwits the cunning fox in this vibrant tale from the Southern states of America. 7–9
Why are there More Questions than Answers, Grandad?	Kenneth Mahood, Picture Puffin/Macmillan
	A book for children, like Sandy, who are always asking questions and for adults who are trying to find answers. 3–8

The Boy Who was Followed Home	Margaret Mahy, Dent Robert, a very ordinary little boy, is followed home by one, then two and finally 43 hippopotamuses! 3–8
The Man Whose Mother was a Pirate	Margaret Mahy, Dent The title says it all! Children will revel in the idea and in the exuberant text and illustrations. 5–10
There's a Nightmare in My Cupboard	Mercer Mayer, Dent An amusing tale to help children explore their fear of the dark and the unknown. 5–11
What a Mess	Frank Muir, illustrated Joseph Wright, Carousel/Benn A funny dog story about a puppy everybody criticizes. 5–11
Peace at Last	Jill Murphy, Macmillan Picturemac Father Bear finds it impossible to sleep, what with Mrs Bear snoring, Baby Bear pretending to be an aeroplane . . . 3–8
Five Minutes' Peace	Jill Murphy, Walker Books Mrs Elephant desperately tries to have five minutes' peace away from her brood of young elephants. A gentle play on a familiar family situation. See also *All in One Piece*. 5–9
Meg and Mog	Helen Nicoll and Jan Pienkowski, Penguin/Heinemann A witch and her cat have trouble getting the witchcraft right with comic results. Numerous other titles to choose from. 3–8
Angry Arthur	Hiawyn Oram, illustrated Satoshi Kitamura, Puffin/Andersen Press Amazing things happen when Arthur's anger explodes. 5–11
Sunshine	Jan Ormerod, Kestrel A wordless picture book story, allowing great scope for language development, showing a small child getting up, waking her parents, having breakfast and getting dressed. The different moods of the morning from relaxed sleepiness to frenzied rush are cleverly captured. *Moonshine* does a similar job with a child going, reluctantly, to bed. 3–8
Smile for Auntie	Diane Paterson, Ernest Benn Children identify with the long-suffering baby who is kissed, cuddled and bribed unsuccessfully by unwelcome auntie. 3–8
The Tiger who Lost his Stripes	Anthony Paul, Sparrow Books Tiger has great difficulty rescuing his stripes from python. 5–11
The Hairy Toe	Emelia Rosato, Blackie A familiar, spooky tale which never fails. The illustrations complement the story well. 5–9
Ironhead	Gerald Rose, Faber/Puffin The fierce, fighting army are overcome by ants. Lots of humour as the soldiers throw off their armour and disappear in their underpants. 5–11
Puss in Boots	Tony Ross, Andersen Press Brightly coloured cartoon drawings provide outrageously funny modern versions of several traditional tales. See also *Jack and the Beanstalk*. 5–11

In the Night Kitchen	Maurice Sendak, Picture Puffin/Bodley Head
	A marvellous imaginary visit to a baker. 5–11
Where the Wild Things are	Maurice Sendak, Picture Puffin/Bodley Head
	Magnificent dream happenings at night – even a wild rumpus – as Max becomes chief of the Wild Things. 3–11
Maisie Middleton	Nita Sowter, Black
	The saucy, bossy small heroine proves much more competent at cooking breakfast than reluctant father. 3–8
My Cat Likes to Hide in Boxes	Eve Sutton, illustrated Lynley Dodd, Puffin/Hamish Hamilton
	A comic poem for infants and everyone else to enjoy. 3–8
The Elephant and the Bad Baby	Elfrida Vitone, Hamish Hamilton/Puffin
	Strong rhythm and repetition in this story about the bad baby 'who never once said *please*'. 3–8
Going West	Martin Waddell, Puffin
	Almost wordless story of the trek to the American West. Most of the detail is left to the skilful, busy illustrations. 3–11
Little Monster	Barrie Wade, illustrated Katinka Kew, Deutsch
	What happens when Mandy overhears her mother talking about her. Will things ever be the same again? 3–8
Dr Xargle's Book of Earthlets	Jeanne Willis, Andersen Press
	The alien view of earth babies and the peculiar things human beings do with them: a view which children will enjoy and appreciate. 5–11
Harry the Dirty Dog	Gene Zion, illustrated Margaret Graham, Picture Puffin/Bodley Head
	Harry, the dog, escapes at bath time and by the time he returns is only just recognizable under the dirt. 5–11

Pop-ups

The Most Amazing Hide-and-Seek Alphabet Book	Robert Crowther, Kestrel
	For each letter of the alphabet there is an animal which pops up, peeps round or climbs out of the appropriate letter as a tab is pulled or turned. Great fun. Then try *The Most Amazing Hide-and-Seek Counting Book*. 3–8
Where's Spot?	Eric Hill, Heinemann/Puffin
	A simple lift-the-flap book for the very young child to search for Spot the dog. ' "Is he behind the door?" "No", says the greedy bear.' Great fun and there are now several Spot books: *Spot's First Walk*, *Spot's Birthday Party*, *Spot's first Christmas*. 3–8
Dinner Time	Jan Pienkowski, Gallery Five
	Each double page spread unfolds to show ferocious looking jaws ready to devour the animal from the previous page. Simple, repetitive text makes this ideal for very young children. 3–8
Haunted House	Jan Pienowski, Heinemann
	A very clever and complex mechanical book to entrance children with spiders, ghosts, skeletons and all sorts of

ingenious horrors being slowly revealed to the unsuspecting reader. *Robot* is a similar and, if anything, even more complex movable book about a family of robots, with the final page launching a rocket into space (well, nearly!).   **5–12**

Collections

The Clothes Horse and Other Stories	Janet and Allan Ahlberg, Kestrel Splendid interpretations of well-known phrases. **7–11**
Stories for Five-Year-Olds	Sara and Stephen Corrin, Faber/Puffin A wealth of stories, traditional and modern, carefully graded for each specific age group, starting with *Stories for Under-Fives* through to *Stories for Ten-Year-Olds* and over **5–11**
The New Golden Land Anthology	Compiled by Judith Elkin, Kestrel An anthology of rhymes, poems, stories, folk tales, ideal for reading aloud in the classroom. **3–11**
How the Whale Became and Other Stories	Ted Hughes, Faber Creation myths told with humour in a forceful, effective way. **7–11**
Seasons of Splendour	Madhur Jaffray, Pavilion Rich collection of Indian tales and legends. **9–13**
The Saga of Erik the Viking	Terry Jones, Puffin A contemporary story capturing the essence of the old Viking sagas. **7–11**
The Horrible Story and Others	Margaret Mahy, Dent 21 short stories by Margaret Mahy provide a treasure trove for reading aloud. **7–11**
Ruth Manning-Sanders Books of. . . .	Methuen/Magnet Collection of folk tales gathered together by subjects: giants, witches, wizards, ghosts, goblins. Ideal for reading aloud. **7–11**
This Little Puffin	Compiled by Elizabeth Mattersen, Puffin An invaluable collection of nursery rhymes, songs and games played with hands and fingers. **3–8**
West Indian Folk Tales	Philip Sherlock, Oxford University Press Amusing, inventive stories with origins in Jamaican folk tales. Try also *Anansi the Spider Man*. **7–11**
The Little Knife who Did all the Work	Alison Uttley, Puffin/Faber Amusing simple tales. **5–8**
Stories for You	Edited by Barrie Wade, Arnold Wheaton A lively collection for reading and reading aloud. **7–11**
Stories for Pleasure	Edited by Barrie Wade, Arnold Wheaton A varied, popular collection of short stories **9–13**

Poetry

I Din Do Nuttin	John Agard, Magnet Simple, accessible poems with a vibrant Caribbean rhythm. See also *Say it Again, Granny*. **5–11**

Please Mrs Butler	Allan Ahlberg, Puffin	
	Humorous poems with a school setting. Guaranteed to be a sure fire success in any classroom.	**5–13**
The Mighty Slide	Allan Ahlberg, Kestrel	
	Five very amusing stories written in verse.	**5–11**
Roger was a Razor Fish	Jill Bennett, Bodley Head/Heinemann	
Tiny Tim	Two short, illustrated collections of poems for younger children, deliberately chosen because their strong rhyme and rhythm make them ideal for children just learning to read.	**3–8**
Earlybirds-Earlywords	Ann and Roger Bonner, Collins	
	Words and pictures work together for enjoyment.	**3–11**
Mother Goose Treasury	Edited by Raymond Briggs, Picture Puffin/Hamish Hamilton	
	Large pages, lavishly illustrated, packed with traditional rhymes collected by Iona and Peter Opie.	**3–8**
The Puffin Book of Magic Verse	Edited by Charles Causley, Puffin	
	A creepy collection.	**7–11**
Figgin Hobbin	Charles Causley, Puffin	
	A varied collection of narrative, comic and thoughtful verse.	**7–11**
Hi-Ran-Ho	Edited by Aidan and Nancy Chambers, Kestrel	
	An illustrated miscellany of verse.	**3–8**
Children as Writers	Heinemann	
	Books of award-winning children's writing published annually. Some splendid poetry (and prose) written by children.	**3–11**
Once Upon a Rhyme	Sara and Stephen Corrin, Faber	
	A range of poetry both traditional and modern to amuse as well as initiate the young child into the world of poetry.	**5–11**
Revolting Rhymes	Roald Dahl, Cape	
Dirty Beasts	Roald Dahl's wickedly funny and often gruesome versions of familiar tales.	**7–11**
A First Poetry Book	John Foster, Oxford University Press	
	Good starter collections for the primary school. See also *A Second Poetry Book, Third . . . , Fourth . . .*	**7–11**
Meet my Folks	Ted Hughes, Faber	
	Funny poems about a funny family.	**7–11**
The Young Puffin Book of Verse	Edited by Barbara Ireson, Puffin	
	A wide ranging, popular and varied collection.	**3–8**
Rhyme Time	Edited Barbara Ireson, Beaver Books	
	A lively collection of verse with much rhyme, repetition and rhythmic patten.	**3–8**
Oh Dinosaur	Barbara Ireson, Corgi/Carousel	
	A collection of animal poems.	**3–8**
The Quangle Wangle's Hat	Edward Lear, Picture Puffin	
	A Noah's ark full of nonsense animals and birds nest in the Quangle Wangle's hat.	**3–11**

Late Home	Brian Lee, Kestrel	
	A collection of poems to stir the imagination, set in town and country.	3–11
What a Morning!	John Longstaff, Gollancz	
	Black spirituals give an unusual angle to the Christmas story.	5–9
You Tell Me	Roger McGough and Michael Rosen, Puffin	
	Simple, funny and fascinating poems about ordinary and intricate events.	7–11
Thoughtscapes	Barry Maybury, Oxford University Press	
	A varied and stimulating collection for older children, illustrated with photographs. See also *Wordscapes*.	8–11
Silly Verse for Kids	Spike Milligan, Puffin	
	A brilliant collection of comic verse. See also *Milliganimiles*.	3–11
Custard and Company	Ogden Nash, Kestrel	
	Ogden Nash's delightful and often eccentric poems gathered together.	5–11
Salford Road	Gareth Owen, Young Lions	
	Evocative poems of urban life. See also *Song of the City*.	7–13
Gargling with Jelly	Brian Patten, Viking/Kestrel	
	A rich collection of funny poems.	7–13
Wouldn't you Like to Know	Michael Rosen, Deutsch	
	Verse that speaks to children in a direct, easy way.	5–11
Mind your own Business	Michael Rosen, Deutsch	
	Verse about children's actual experiences, feelings and imaginings.	3–11
You Can't Catch Me!	Michael Rosen, Deutsch/Puffin	
	Picture book version of Michael Rosen's delightfully humorous poems for younger children.	3–8
Hairy Tales and Nursery Crimes	Michael Rosen, Deutsch	
	An amusing collection of punning poems and tales, based on familiar fairy tales and nursery rhyme characters.	5–10
Speech Rhymes	Edited by Clive Sanson, Black	
	A collection to give pleasure in sound and rhythm – essential to read aloud.	3–8
I'll Tell you a Tale	Ian Seraillier, Puffin	
	An illustrated selection of rhymes, jokes and stories about places and people.	7–11
Mother Goose Comes to Cable Street	Rosemary Stones and Andrew Mann, Picture Puffin	
	Traditional nursery rhymes given a modern inner-city feel through Dan Jones's illustrations.	3–11
All Sorts of Poems	Edited by Ann Thwaite, Methuen	
	A modern miscellany of poems by various writers.	7–11
The Giant Jam Sandwich	J. Vernon and Janet Burroway, Piccolo	
	An enchanting story poem about a swarm of wasps that settles on a village.	3–11

Conkers	Barrie Wade, Oxford University Press
	A varied collection of poems about school, growing up and the experience of childhood. **7–12**
Young Verse	Edited by Julia Watson, Armada Lion
	Strange events, people and creatures in verse for young people. **5–11**
Stanley Bagshaw and the Fourteen-foot Wheel	Bob Wilson, Puffin/Hamish Hamilton
	Verse and cartoon pictures tell the tale of Stanley who helps out at the local factory, with fantastic results. **7–11**
I Like this Poem	Edited by Kaye Webb, Puffin
	An anthology of poems chosen by children together with reasons for their choices. **3–11**
Rabbiting on	Kit Wright, Fontana Lions
	A popular book of poems about attitudes, events, people and things. See also *Hot Dog* and other poems (Kestrel) and *Cat among the Pigeons* (Kestrel). **7–11**

Fiction

Happy Families series	Allan Ahlberg, Kestrel
	Amusing stories to read aloud or for early readers, especially *Mrs Plug the Plumber*, *Mrs Wobble the Waitress*, *Miss Brick the Builder's Baby*. **5–9**
Arabel's Raven	Joan Aiken, BBC
	Hilarious stories about Arabel and her pet raven, Mortimer. **6–9**
A Bear Called Paddington, etc.	Michael Bond, Puffin/Collins
	Popular, enjoyable, funny stories about a bear who constantly causes turmoil. Then try *Paddington Helps out*, *Paddington Marches on*, *Here Comes Thursday*. **6–11**
Flat Stanley	Jeff Brown and Tomi Ungerer, Penguin/Methuen
	There are advantages in being only half an inch thick – slipping under doors for instance! A comic book of adventure. **6–9**
The Secret Garden	Frances Hodgson Burnett, Puffin/Heinemann
	The discovery of a mysterious garden creates a whole new future for two lonely children. **7–11**
The Julian Stories	Ann Cameron, Gollancz
	Charming short stories about two scampish black children. The stories read aloud well. Try also *More Stories Julian Tells*. **5–11**
Sunshine Island, Moonshine Bay	Clare Cherrington, Collins
	Warm stories with a Caribbean setting. **7–11**
Ramona Books	Beverly Cleary, Puffin
	The innocent and irrepressible Ramona is experiencing the mysteries of school for the first time. Familiar yet sometimes catastrophic misunderstandings have a great appeal to young readers. **6–9**
A Gift from Winklesea	Helen Cresswell, Puffin/Brockhampton

It is not every parent that receives such an unusual present
from a seaside holiday! Then try *The Piemakers*.

Storm	Kevin Crossley-Holland, Heinemann	
	A simple yet haunting ghost story.	7–11
Charlie and the Chocolate Factory	Roald Dahl, Puffin	
	A popular, lively narrative.	6–11
Fantastic Mr Fox	Roald Dahl, Puffin	
	A popular story of a fox and the human beings who are no match for his brilliant cunning.	6–11
James and the Giant Peach	Roald Dahl, Puffin/Allen and Unwin	
	Fantastic adventures after James's controlling adults are removed. Then try *Charlie and the Great Glass Elevator*, *Danny the Champion of the World*.	7–11
The BFG	Ronald Dahl, Cape	
	The Big Friendly Giant (BFG) befriends tiny bespectacled Sophie and rids the world of the flesh-eating giants. Very funny. Try also *The Witches*.	7–11
My Naughty Little Sister, etc.	Dorothy Edwards, Puffin/Methuen	
	Lively stories which appeal to nursery and infant age groups especially.	4–8
Bridget and William	Jane Gordan, Hamish Hamilton/Puffin	
	Two very short, gripping stories about girls and their horses.	6–9
Kit in Boots	Jane Gordan, Julia MacRae Books	
	A tale of a small child on a remote Welsh farm.	7–11
The Weirdstone of Brisingamen	Alan Garner, Collins	
	A gripping fantasy story of children against the powers of evil set in Alderley Edge. Then try *The Moon of Gomrath*, *Elidor*.	8–11
The Shrinking of Treehorn	Florence Parry Heide, Puffin	
	Well, adults *do* sometimes ignore children and this brilliant book strikes a chord with young readers (and younger listeners). Then try *Treehorn's Treasure*.	6–11
The Iron Man	Ted Hughes, Faber	
	A modern myth brilliantly told.	6–11
Chips and Jessie	Shirley Hughes, Bodley Head	
	Part comic strip, part straight narrative, highly individual and amusingly accessible short stories. Follow with *Another Helping of Chips*.	7–11
Who's a Clever Girl, Then?	Rose Impey, Heinemann	
	A small girl joins a gang of pirates and refuses stereotyped roles.	7–11
Finn Family Moomintroll	Tove Jansson, Puffin	
	Popular stories of adventure and mystery set in Moominland.	7–11
Tales from Allotment Street	Margaret Joy, Faber	
	Simple, unpretentious stories for and about infant school children.	5–9

The Turbulent Term of Tyke Tyler	Gene Kemp, Puffin Very funny story of life in a primary school. **8–12**
Stig of the Dump	Clive King, Puffin Stone-age Stig comes to a modern scene. Try also *Snakes and Snakes*. **7–11**
ESP	Dick King-Smith, Marilyn Malin Books ESP the pigeon crash lands on Smelly the tramp in this light-hearted story. See also *Yob* and *Lightning Fred*. **7–11**
A Wizard of Earthsea	Ursula LeGuin, Puffin/Gollancz First title in an imaginative fantasy trilogy for young readers. Then try *The Tombs of Atuan*, *The Farthest Shore*. **8–12**
The Lion, the Witch and the Wardrobe	C. S. Lewis, Puffin/Macmillan Good and evil conflict in the fabulous land of Narnia where four children engage in dangerous, heroic exploits. **7–11**
All about the Bullerby Children	Astrid Lindgren, Puffin Adventure stories about a group of children. Eminently readable. Try also *Pippi Longstocking*. **7–11**
The Ghost of Thomas Kempe	Penelope Lively, Piccolo 10-year-old James is blamed for the mischief done by the ghosts of a 17th-century sorcerer. A humorous trip into the supernatural. **8–12**
Frog and Toad Together	Arnold Lobel, Worlds Work Hilarious tales about easy-going Frog and his volatile friend, Toad, ideal for children just learning to read. Also *Frog and Toad are Friends* and *Frog and Toad all Year*. **5–11**
No More School	William Mayne, Puffin/Hamish Hamilton What happens when a group of children take over the organization of school. Then try *A Swarm in May*. **6–11**
The Railway Children	Edith Nesbit, Puffin/Ernest Benn Adventures of London children who move to the countryside near the railway. **8–12**
Bedknobs and Broomsticks	Mary Norton, Puffin/Dent An imaginative, amusing, powerful story with fascinating characters. Then try *The Borrowers*. **8–12**
The Battle of Bubble and Squeak	Philippa Pearce, Puffin The battle is between the children and their mother who would do anything to get rid of the two gerbils, Bubble and Squeak. **8–12**
A Dog So Small	Philippa Pearce, Puffin A popular story of a boy's yearning for a dog. **8–12**
What the Neighbours Did	Philippa Pearce, Puffin/Longman Imaginative and sensitive stories about their neighbourhood. Then try *Tom's Midnight Garden*. **8–12**
101 Dalmatians	Dodie Smith, Puffin A popular story of the great dog rescue as good (Pongo and Missis) and evil (Cruella de Vil) battle for Dalmatian prisoners. Try also *The Starlight Barking*. **8–11**
Puss and Cat	Catherine Storr, Faber

	A lively, compelling adventure story focusing on the twins, Puss and Cat, their similarities and differences. Try also *Robin*. 7–11
The Chief's Daughter	Rosemary Sutcliff, Piccolo/Hamish Hamilton An adventure story full of danger and incident. Try also *Shifting Sands*, *The Truce of the Games*. 7–11
The Ice Palace	Robert Swindells, Antelope A heroic and imaginative tale of rescue from the cruel Starjik who kidnaps children. 8–12
Worzel Gummidge	Barbara Todd, Puffin A well-known character, popular with children, who gets into a variety of adventures. 7–11
The Hobbit	J. R. R. Tolkien Penguin/Allen and Unwin A brilliantly told, imaginative story of heroic adventure in the land of hobbits and dragons. Try also *The Lord of the Rings*. 8–12
Top of the World	John Rowe Townsend, Puffin/Cambridge University Press Top of the world is the roof of a block of flats and Donald refuses to come down. Try also *Pirate's Island*. 8–12
A Question of Honour	Ann Wade, Arnold Wheaton Vividly illustrated retelling of the story of Rama and Sita. The ten-headed demon strikes! Try also the colourful collections of folk tales and legends from many lands in *Around the World*, *Far and Wide*, *Worldly Wise*, *A Far Cry*, *Timeless Tales*, *Eastern Promise*, *Larger than Life*, stories of the elements in *Earth*, *Air*, *Fire and Water* and the creation stories in *When Time Began*. 8–12
Imogen the Brave	Barrie Wade, Arnold Wheaton Only a girl like Imogen is clever enough to outwit the dreadful monster Handclaw. Try also *Cinnabar Summer*. 7–11
Beowulf	Barrie Wade, Arnold Wheaton A superbly illustrated, gripping retelling of the powerful legend. Then try *A Test of Truth* (Sir Gawain and the Green Knight) and the King Arthur stories retold in three books *Paths of Glory*, *For Love and Honour* and *End of an Era*. 8–12
Charlotte's Web	E. B. White, Puffin A splendid story – moving and comic – about a spider's love and care for her friend Wilbur, the pig. Then try *The Trumpet of the Swan*. 8–12
The Little House in the Big Woods	Laura Ingalls Wilder, Puffin/Methuen First of the books about Laura's adventures in a tough, primitive community. Then try *Little House on the Prairie*, etc. 8–12
Gobbolino the Witch's Cat	Ursula Moray Williams, Puffin/Harrap A lively story about a cat desperately trying to be ordinary but with too much skill for his own good. Try also *The Adventures of the Little Wooden Horse*. 8–12

Supergran	Forest Wilson, Puffin
	Supergran is a bouncy, comic senior citizen with super
	powers. 8–12

Information books written in story form

Ananda in Sri Lanka	Carol Baker, Hamish Hamilton
	A story of Buddhism and a child's experience of life in a Sri
	Lankan village. 5–11
A Farm in the City	Olivia Bennett, Hamish Hamilton
	The story of a visit to a city farm by a group of children. See
	also *A Turkish Afternoon, The Albany Road Mural.* 5–11
Suzy	Elizabeth Chapman, illustrated Margery Gill, Bodley Head
	The illustrated story of Suzy, a partially sighted girl, who
	enjoys life to the full. One of a special situation series. 5–11
Japanese Family	Judith Elkin, Black
	12-year-old Daisuke talks about his life in Tokyo living with
	his parents and brother. 8–13
Roman Villa	Brian Davison, Hamish Hamilton
	An illustrated story of life in Roman Britain. 7–11
Terrible Claw: The Story of a Carnivorous Dinosaur	Beverly Halstead, Collins
	The life cycle of a dinosaur in story form, with often gory
	illustrations. See also *A Brontosaur: the Life Story*
	Unearthed. 6–11
Paul in Hospital	Camilla Jessel, Methuen
	Simple narrative about a boy's stay in hospital. Try also *Mark's*
	Wheelchair Adventures. 5–11
Oak and Company	Richard Mabey, Kestrel
	A beautiful, illustrated story of the oak tree from its beginning
	as an acorn 200 years ago to the night when it is struck by
	lightning. 7–11
Sweet-Tooth Sunil	Joan Solomon, Hamish Hamilton
	The story of Sunil and Sonia who prepare for the Hindu
	Festival of Lights. See also *Gifts and Almonds, A Present for*
	Mom, Bobbi's New Year. 5–11
Gandhi	Kathryn Spink, Hamish Hamilton
	The story of the great man – another in the *Profiles* series of
	illustrated biographies. 7–11
The Postman	Anne Stewart, Hamish Hamilton
	All the Cherrystones series show what it's like to do a
	particular job. The postman works in Birmingham. 5–11
Linda Goes to Hospital	Barrie Wade, Black
	A colour photographic record of a child's stay in hospital with
	accompanying narrative. A 7 year old wrote the first draft.
	Other titles include *Simon Goes to the Optician, Jessica Goes to*
	the Dentist, Wayne is Adopted. 5–11
Jimmy Goes to the Dentist	Barrie Wade, Hamish Hamilton
	A colour photographic narrative of dental treatment
	embodying the findings of modern dental research but written
	for primary age children. 5–11

PART FOUR

Writing to read

7 Developing contexts for writing narrative

LENA STRANG

> Of devices for teaching writing, there is no end; and most if not all of them cripple the mind and deform the body. Thank God, the method of teaching children to speak was invented before the schoolmaster appeared!
>
> Francis W. Parker, *Talks on Pedagogics: An Outline of the Theory of Concentration*, New York, Barnes, 1890

The problem

Double English with the fourth years in my secondary school on Monday morning was something that I never looked forward to. It probably had everything to do with my difficulties in managing to enthuse the pupils or persuading them to work purposefully on tasks which I presented. Their written course work was unremarkable and barely fulfilled the criteria for the two-year course to a leaver's qualification. The pupils were not used to the processes of drafting and were hard pressed to modify any work handed in for assessment.

The class was not unlike many other fourth years in multicultural inner city areas. Among the 22 pupils the majority were Asian and their community languages included Urdu, Panjabi, Gujurati and Bengali. There were also 3 Afro-Caribbean and 2 white pupils. Potentially, ample opportunity existed for developing work drawn from the pupils' diverse backgrounds but the reality of hostility and disaffection on the part of many pupils made this difficult, fuelled no doubt by the administrative measures taken by the school to deal with the problems. Continuity in the classroom was frequently disrupted by spells of suspensions. Why work hard in the classroom anyway? Many of the pupils were only marking time, while others were predicted not to accomplish more than a string of failures in examinations.

It was more an act of self-preservation that induced me to embark on an ambitious story-writing project. Earlier in the year the class had worked on a Caribbean story which involved prediction and completion of the narrative in play form to be recorded and displayed. Carlton, who had not produced any coursework yet, dictated a highly sophisticated and apt dialogue in Creole for his partner to write down. The plays were recorded, scripts typed up and displayed with extracts published in the school magazine. I had not anticipated the effect this work would have on the class. Carlton cherished his role as 'language consultant', while the prospect of having an audience seemed to spur the pupils on. The pupils were more willing to redraft their work and took pleasure in seeing their work in print.

I was interested in trying to determine to what extent an element of writing for a real audience influences the process of writing. I suspect that much of the writing that takes place in the classroom is seen as irrelevant by many pupils since there is no immediate purpose or identifiable audience. There is very often no genuine context, with writing aimed at the teacher or for the purpose of recording facts. The tasks set are often insufficiently defined and an air of vagueness tends to surround the whole concept of how children learn to write. Barnes *et al.* (1969) observed that young writers are often at a loss when confronted with typical written assignments at school (p.164).

> The tasks frequently seem to lack a clear function, nor do they seem to leave room for the expression of the writer's own ideas and his way of seeing things. All too rarely in school written assignments is the writer expressing something he wants to say to others.

In recent years much more consideration has been given to the optimum conditions for the best writing. The context in which the learning takes place is considered crucial for any success in writing. A specific audience for writing is stressed: 'More confident and competent writers develop when the writing performed is for a specific audience and purpose; where the child has control over *what* is written, *why* and for *whom* (Schools Curriculum Development Committee 1988, p.2).

Would a more ambitious project involving writing for a genuine audience motivate the pupils to write and help them to become more proficient writers? I was prepared to hazard a 'yes'. With the help of a local story teller and a member of the city's multicultural education faculty assigned to the school and with whom I was team teaching, the story-writing project was begun.

What were our aims? We wanted the pupils to write story books for children in local junior and infant schools. We wanted the pupils to meet the children they were writing for and be encouraged to negotiate and adapt their writing in response to the needs and specifications of their reading and listening 'clients'. We hoped they would be able to share their experience of narrative and increase their understanding of the characteristics of texts through the variety of models presented to them. Perhaps they would become better story tellers themselves as possible future parents. The nature of the work could encourage closer co-operation and capitalize on specific expertise (I knew, for instance, that two of the pupils were excellent artists). We could explore racial and gender stereotyping in books and provide opportunities for pupils to write in their community languages. The work with the junior schools could be a mutually beneficial experience. We thought that the end-products, the printed story books, written by older pupils might be of value for reading with younger children. Above all, we hoped the work would give the pupils a sense of purpose and be a way of demonstrating that they can succeed. By writing stories that would be read by real readers the pupils would develop a sense of being authors and realize the interconnection between reading and writing.

The project was to run for the whole of the summer term and a double lesson a week was set aside. In fact, when the work developed, additional time had to be spent on it. We had great difficulties initially in 'selling' the project to the pupils who were not convinced about the validity of the work. To many of them the amount of talking and reading involved did not constitute real work, particularly as the parallel classes were getting on with the serious business of exam folder work. The fact that the stories could be used for coursework assessment provided some reassurance. It is interesting to note here the extent to which traditional ways of working dominate the expectations of pupils (and teachers) and the resistance that alternative approaches can meet with.

Throughout the project the pupils were encouraged to browse and to borrow story books brought into the classroom and to exchange their own experiences of reading and telling stories. We invited a sixth-form student to tell stories in Urdu in order to encourage and validate the use of community languages. While some of the pupils were prepared to tell stories in other languages, none of them felt they were able to write stories in other than English. However, several of the stories were later translated into Urdu and Panjabi by sixth-form students. Pupils were also urged to try out stories on younger sisters and brothers. This met with varying success as some pupils reported later.

'My brother liked the story and he joined in as well.'
'They enjoyed it but soon got bored.'
'They were too young to understand it.'
'He wasn't listening really.'

A speaker as well as a story teller needs to adapt to the requirements of the listener. Similarly, a writer needs to respond to the needs of the reader although the influence is not as immediate or as direct. We wanted the students to make this connection in their own story telling and writing.

During our visits to the two junior schools we had chosen, the pupils were able to meet the children they were writing for and observe the reactions as teachers told them stories. Two of the pupils told the group stories in Urdu, while a boy reciprocated by telling a story in Gujurati using props and a cardboard cut-out of a greedy cat!

Later the pupils compiled a 'brainstorm' list of their thoughts about stories and the children they had observed:

- They like stories to be exciting and have a happy ending.
- They like stories to do with adventures, cars and animals.
- They can learn about other countries and the world outside.

- They like stories before they go to bed.
- Stories often have a moral at the end.
- Stories make words easier to understand.
- Stories make their vocabulary better.
- Pictures make a story more interesting.

The pupils obviously had an expectation of stories derived from their own knowledge of the genre. They would now have to try to match their own writing to this expectation.

Other observations were made about the techniques used by the story teller to sustain the interest of the children.

> The storyteller used her hands, getting the children to repeat the words. They liked looking at the pictures which made the story more interesting and the kids joined in. She aroused the children's curiosity . . .

> The use of hands was very good because people who haven't got much English vocab. will understand the movement of the hands . . . Using props can make a boring story very lively . . . The voice control was very good and interested the children and kept them awake.

Knowledge of genre

How did talking to the children, finding out what kind of stories they liked and analysing the children's reactions to the stories they were told, affect the pupils' own story writing? Abdullah, who later developed into a skilled story teller, co-wrote *The Ghost Train* with Carlton. In a subsequent recorded evaluation session the following transpired:

Teacher: Did you have anyone in mind when you were writing it?
Abdullah: No . . .
Teacher: Because yours had more difficult language in it, did you think about who you were writing for?
Abdullah: No, not really.
Carlton: He just writ it.
Abdullah: I didn't think much about the audience because when you actually read out your story you can change the words according to the ages of the audience.

Although he does not perhaps realize it, Abdullah has a clear idea of the genre of stories. His own story adheres very closely to established conventions and draws on his knowledge of texts, which demonstrates the importance of children learning and internalizing genres for their own writing. As Gunther Kress (1982) observes (p.99):

> The child has to gain mastery over the forms and possibilities of the different generic types, as part of the process of learning to write. . . . The achievement of genre is a necessary and integral part of the achievement of writing; the two are inextricably linked.

A 'sense of audience' can, however, be an elusive concept as it is not always clear what exactly it refers to. It does not fully account for the skilled writer's ability to write appropriately for intended audiences. Frank Smith (1982a) maintains that (p.80):

> Effective writing is writing that meets the conventional demands of the text, demands that impose themselves on both writers and readers . . . The text itself – the task at hand – is the primary concern. In other words, between the author and audience is always a specific task, the task of writing an appropriate text in an appropriate register.

Smith argues that choosing the appropriate register for the intended audience becomes, in fact, the crucial factor in effective writing. I think the pupils were able to write effectively because they knew the conventional demands of the writing and they were writing for a specific audience who shared these expectations.

Abdullah was later asked in a television news bulletin featuring the project, what he thought made a good story. His response was:

> You need a witch, a new world which will keep the children interested . . . somewhere where the children can think and imagine what the place is like . . . keep the imagination going . . . and you need a little man who is very strange.

The fact that Abdullah managed to keep his audience spell-bound when telling his story demonstrates that apart from his story-telling skills, he and also his audience recognized it had all the essential ingredients for a good children's story. Both he and his audience share a 'sense of the conventional written register' (Smith 1982a, p.80).

While other pupils adhered to similar conventions of genre they were, however, more inclined to make modifications to their work as a direct result of contact with their audience. Some had already begun writing their stories before the first visit to the junior schools. It was interesting to note that much alteration took place afterwards and, in fact, several stories were discarded altogether. Rajinder had problems with his story and rejected his first attempt as being 'too complicated'. He decided that his story about a lion who changed into a tiger was inappropriate ('. . . there was something wrong with it. I couldn't change it') and he ended up writing his own modified version of *Billy and the Beanstalk!* The fact that Rajinder and some of the other pupils decided to take on elements from well-known children's stories does not in any way detract from their achievement. They have learnt the conventions and apply their knowledge about stories appropriately.

Another pupil was concerned that the language he used 'was not too hard for the children . . . I thought of them a lot. I wanted to make sure the children would react in a good way . . . I had found out how the children reacted when a story was read to them.' Pakhan had earlier observed the junior school teacher tell a story about a big turnip where a considerable amount of repetition had been used. He noticed how involved the children became and how eagerly they joined in.

Just then in front of them stood a small man.

All of a sudden there was a big bang and they found themselves in another world. Paul was shaken up and looked at John in shock. "What has happened?" they wondered. Just then in front of them stood a small man. He looked very strange to them because of his height and the colour of his hair. He really looked unusual!

Figure 7.1 A little man

Jack and the Princess

by Rita Pankhania and Arfah Tasneem

Figure 7.2   Jack and the Princess

Teacher: What I liked about your story was the repetition.
Pakhan: Ah . . .
Teacher: Well, when the giraffe gets stuck in the hole all the animals try to help and you said first the tiger pulled and then the monkey pulled and then the lion pulled . . . Now where did you get that idea from?
Pakhan: I got that idea from another book about a turnip, a big turnip.
Abdullah: Oh, yes that's right!!
Pakhan: Yes, I thought the children would get it . . . think about that and come to an understanding about it.

Pakhan, along with many of the other pupils, was able to generalize from particular kinds of texts and take on these characteristics in his own writing.

The ending of *Why the Giraffe Got his Long Neck* proved unsatisfactory. Pakhan was unhappy about it and wanted to try it out on other pupils in the class who then suggested alternative endings. The willingness to modify and critically assess their own writing based on criteria which they had by now established was striking. I remembered the reluctance with which any suggestions for rewriting work had been met earlier. Now the impetus for redrafting, or in some cases starting the work all over again, came from the pupils themselves. They wanted their products to be 'right' and did not feel demoralized if they had to make several attempts.

We also wanted the pupils to be aware of the gender and racial stereotyping which is inherent in many traditional tales. As a result many pupils included strong female characters in their stories. In one story called *Jack and the Princess* the characters behave in predictable ways but while Jack is dressed as a traditional miller's son, Laila is an Indian princess dressed in a beautiful sari. In one version Goldilocks is really Supergirl in disguise and at the end it is Supergran that saves the day! In an alternative version, the bears terrorized by Goldilocks turn to Red Riding Hood for help who then proceeds to outwit them all! These two stories remained favourites among the junior school class the pupils later visited.

The seemingly insurmountable problems of illustrating the stories were eventually overcome with advice from art teachers and with pupils helping each other to a much greater extent than previously. During lessons characterized by a hectic workshop atmosphere, the stories were typed up, captions letrasetted, covers designed and books bound, all just in time for our final visit to the junior schools at the end of the term. This was the pinnacle of the project as the pupils were able to go into the schools with their printed books and present them to the children they had been writing for. Many of the pupils felt by now confident enough to tell groups of children their stories and the ones that felt too apprehensive were helped out by the teachers. To the delight of the authors, one child was heard to remark, 'We really had some nice stories today, didn't we?'

The benefits

For the majority of the pupils, the project had a marked effect. By having a real audience of readers and listeners for their writing, a sense of purpose was instilled. The pupils had the motivation and remarkable patience to produce meticulous work of high standard. We were able to utilize a variety of talents in the class. Pupils who were skilled at artwork were in great demand, the story tellers could excel and the bilingual students could demonstrate that they had a worthwhile talent.

It was important for the students to gain an understanding of the whole process involved in writing – from initial consultations with clients, planning, drafting and redrafting to the completion of the end-product. Our production difficulties and lack of technical back up were, in fact, turned to our advantage. More out of necessity, the pupils had to be involved in all the stages of production including letrasetting, pagination, photocopying and binding. Later in a radio programme Pakhan assessed what aspect of the project had been most important to him: 'I enjoyed actually planning the books, binding them, drawing the pictures for them . . . really the total process.'

Being engaged in story writing and coming to see themselves increasingly as authors, helped to demystify writing and the whole business of book production. Because of the demands generated for material of this kind in junior schools, the books were later marketed commercially through the school project centre, involving the authors and pupils in other subject areas.

The sense of pride and achievement was never more obvious as when one of

Figure 7.3   Sharing the book

the 'non-exam' pupils first held his printed book in his hand. Abdullah shared this satisfaction.

> I've learnt it's not as easy as it looks, it's a lengthy process . . . but when the actual book is finished, it's great to see your book lying there and the children enjoying it – that's the greatest part of it all – the children enjoying the stories.

The effects of success carried over to other areas of work. On the whole, attendance improved markedly and the improved quality of the pupils' folder work was a direct consequence of the project. It was also interesting to note the increasing motivation of boys in a curriculum area where they had traditionally underachieved in comparison to girls.

During their fifth year at school, the pupils were increasingly involved in dissemination of the project. Groups of pupils took part in television and radio programmes and were participants in numerous teacher workshops and conferences. It was amazing to see the maturity and the confidence with which the pupils discussed their work with teachers.

The readers

The benefits of the project to the older pupils are clear, but what about the readers? What did they gain from the partnership? Firstly, they obviously gained the enjoyment which is necessary to sustain young readers. Secondly, they put language to use for a variety of purposes.

They engaged in dialogue, they listened to stories being read and in turn were able to read stories aloud – helping them to develop a sense of difference between spoken and written language. They gained an awareness that writing is for reading and may also have been assisted as developing readers and writers themselves.

As John Richmond (1985) says:

> Writing is nurtured by experience of texts – by reading. If speech is the prime activity which grants meaning, reading is the daily evidence that writing exists and has been done; the reader can become a writer. The reader/writer sorts the evidence, for instance, of a spelling system, of conventions of punctuation, of the tone of voice which distinguishes fairy story from fire warning notice, of the use of rhythm, rhyme and repetition in verse, of the various ways writers order their text when recounting an experience or expressing a point of view. In other words, a large proportion of the detailed learning which developing writers need to do is done as a result of seeing the achievement of others.

It was important for the older pupils to be seen to be achieving and so providing models of behaviour for younger ones to emulate. Similarly, it was important for ethnic minority children to see pupils from their own communities in status roles and for community languages to be used for real educational purposes, not merely as token gestures.

As the frequent orders for the story books demonstrated, there is a need for 'real' books in junior schools which do away with traditional stereotypes inherent in many graded readers, real narratives which are cheap and accessible and are written in ways to which young children can relate.

8 Developing contexts for writing non-narrative

VALERIE CHERRINGTON

Barriers to understanding

Whereas readers frequently ask about a novel, a poem or a play 'Is it true?', information and textbooks have acquired such a mystique that young readers rarely question them. To be an active interrogator of the text of such a non-fiction book the reader must understand the information it contains. There are, however, at least three barriers to such understanding, the main one being located in the books themselves.

Difficulty of language and organization

Many children who can read and enjoy narratives still have difficulty in understanding their school textbooks and the information books they use for project work. The less familiar, more varied and complex linguistic structures of non-narrative texts frequently cause comprehension problems for learners. These structures do not form part of our oral culture and if young children neither read non-fiction texts nor hear them read aloud they are at a disadvantage. When they first encounter these texts in school, they cannot form predictions about their structures as they can in their reading of stories.

Non-fiction (see Perera 1986) is frequently not ordered chronologically, is less personal, entails more 'information processing' and is syntactically more complex than narrative reading. Books already densely packed with information frequently contain complex subject noun phrases.

> *The kind of dark coal that is found in Wales and which is hard and slow burning* is called anthracite.

Here the young reader has a deal of information to carry forward until the verb is reached and the sense completed. Additional problems are caused by the way whole books are constructed (grouping apparently random facts together, lengthy and complex explanations interleaved with simpler passages of instruction) and by the requirement of familiarity with conventions such as contents and index.

Reading for learning also calls for reflective reading. Exciting stories read for pleasure can be understood with relatively little effort but, as Lunzer and Gardner (1984) point out, most children expect the same thing to apply to all reading. However, non-narrative texts, densely packed with information, and with more difficult language, require that readers form a habit of pausing to reflect upon the overall sense of what they are reading.

Difficulty of finding appropriate non-narrative materials

There is a shortage of suitable information books for the primary age range, the problem being particularly noticeable at the lower end of the age range and for less able readers. Criticisms, (e.g. Heeks 1982; Meek 1977; Lavender 1983 and Paice 1984) have been made about illustrations, organization, accuracy and subject coverage, lack of literary merit and personal tone to promote interest and excitement as well as the difficult language referred to above.

Difficulty of information retrieval

Children do not naturally acquire the skills necessary to carry out research work properly. They need teaching to read for different purposes: to skim, to scan, to scrutinize. They require help with all kinds of information-retrieval, note making, cross-referencing and with ordering information for different purposes. Project work is sometimes approached without any real sense of purpose and becomes simply a fact-gathering exercise. Unless children see the work as having a valid purpose and unless they are encouraged to pose pertinent questions, almost anything about a topic is worth writing about and copying verbatim may seem adequate.

A good deal of writing done in the name of 'project work' amounts to no more than reproducing large, undigested chunks of books. As HMI point out (DES 1982) 'copying kept the children busy and produced work of an apparently reasonable standard, but it did not promote real progress in language development, or reveal what the children had remembered or understood' (p.12).

One way forward

One way of solving these three related difficulties in project work is to create an information book with teacher and children working together to find information and compose a text using children's own language. This collaborative work exploits the close and vital relationship between reading and writing, since anything done to support and develop reading will support and develop writing and vice versa; helps to fill 'gaps' in the present information book supply and build up readable non-fiction book collections; and provides a meaningful context in which to teach and develop information skills. Each stage of the process of writing an information book generates a great deal of talk, listening and reading for various purposes and provides many other learning opportunities and valuable experiences. Such a project can satisfy many needs, often simultaneously.

One example of information-book writing by children has been described and can be found in *Talking to Some Purpose* (Wade *et al.* 1985). This case study involved a group of 8–9-year-old boys of lower reading ability who, unable to find any books they could read about 'how cars are made', decided to write their own with the help of their teacher.

The remainder of this chapter describes how a group of four junior school girls aged 8–9 years set about the process of writing their own information book through collaborative talk and inquiry with their teacher.

Amy and Sue were considered very intelligent and hard working. Denise was considered lazy and underachieving while Linda was considered the least able academically and rather unsure of herself.

Preliminary activities

Topic, purpose and audience

The children decided to find out about cruelty to animals in captivity, in zoos and circuses. Their purpose was to write a book exposing the cruelty that they felt existed and their specific, intended audience was children of their own age. From the beginning, therefore, they were immersed in a realistic task to argue a case.

The only available children's book which dealt with the 'cruelty' aspect of zoos and circuses was *The Use and Abuse of Animals* (Richmond-Watson 1984) – and since that was intended for older children the text was too difficult.

Using sources of information

Information was gathered from the following sources:

- their own experience and knowledge.
- children's library – book title supplied.
- picture library – pictures.
- adult lending section – books.
- reference library – photocopied texts and several useful addresses.
- RSPCA – booklets, pamphlets and project kits.
- Circus Fans' Association of Great Britain – magazine and other literature.
- local newspaper article and subsequent telephone conversation with author.
- a zoo – children visited the zoo and interviewed the education officer.

The children encountered different points of view and found the need to evaluate information and distinguish between fact and opinion. They found out how difficult it can be to get at the truth where controversial issues are concerned.

Circuses

Written texts were the only sources of information available for this phase. Most were intended for adults and even the few texts intended for children were quite difficult for 8–9 year olds. Therefore support was required at all stages, including the following:

Locating information

As the teacher explained what she was doing when she involved the children in the search for information, opportunities arose to learn about:

- overviewing books – use of cover, title, list of contents, index, chapter headings, subheadings.
- alphabetical order.

Reading strategies

Again, the teacher explained what she was doing and encouraged the children in:

- scanning lists, e.g. indexes.
- skimming pages – to locate required information.
- intensive reading – when required information was thought to have been located (for the children this also involved intensive listening as the teacher read aloud).

Comprehending the written texts

The children required substantial support in understanding and extracting information from the difficult texts but their high motivation helped to sustain attention. The collaborative nature of the task generated a great deal of talk and encouraged pausing for reflection.

Texts were tackled in various ways. For example, the teacher read the text aloud (helping pupils to re-create its meaning) as clearly and expressively as possible and then discussed it with the children (see Figure 8.1 page 145). This strategy allowed for exploration and consideration of such things as:

- main headings and subheadings.
- main ideas, supporting details.
- interpreting dense and complex language, enabling children to discuss the information and then be in a better position to ask questions, answer questions and write in their own words.

Some words had to be explained and discussed, for example, 'signals', 'respond', 'aggression'.

It was important for the children to make sense of the information by relating it to experiences in their own lives. For example, Amy talked about how she used her outstretched hand as a signal for training her rabbit:

Amy: I / got some bread and some rabbit food and put him a long way away / and then / I held my hand out and he used to run.

Drama was frequently used for learning and was initiated spontaneously by both teacher and children, for example to demonstrate how animals are trained. The children often suggested making up plays. The children had a sense of purpose which led to selective note taking. Whenever possible they were encouraged to underline or label information they wanted to use (see italics in Figure 8.1).

During the supported reading sessions the teacher would sometimes ask the children to express the ideas in simpler language – as a rehearsal for writing for their intended audience, e.g. 'I've just thought/sometimes tigers or lions / tigers or lions / get / get ready to fight people if they get / um / afraid'.

To have made the children struggle through every difficult text would have been tedious and too time consuming, so sometimes the teacher expressed the text in simpler language either orally or in writing and discussed it with the children.

Sometimes the children were asked to search for information on their own, with parents' help or in pairs and then to write notes in language that their intended audience would understand. These findings were then reported to the rest of the group and discussed.

Frequently discussion centred on the precise meaning of words, as when they considered whether to use the word 'confused'.

Linda: It's when it gets / when you get all muddled up and you don't know what you're doing.
Sue: Muddled seems a bit funny though.

The teacher was surprised by Linda's competent explanation of 'confused', and when she checked to see if they understood *why* some dolphins were confused Linda explained that very well too:

Linda: Because the walls are echoing and they think it's another dolphin mimicking them / and they get all confused and that.

It is doubtful whether this 'less able' child would reveal the same degree of comprehension and the same ability to explain without the opportunity to put language to use for purposes and an audience that were clear to her.

Recording, storing and organizing information

Immediately after each session of discussing a text the children were asked to select and record relevant information in language that their intended audience would understand. This automatically discouraged verbatim copying. Their audience was constantly being considered, for example:

> *Denise:* On the arrival of the small elephants they have to/um . . .
> *Amy:* They won't understand what 'on arrival' means.

It would have taken too long for the children to discuss and take notes from every difficult text so the teacher made some notes for them.

The need to synthesize information from different sources also lessened the possibility of verbatim copying when the actual text was being composed (see below). The following procedure made it easier to collate, organize and cope with a large amount of information.

Recording the information/making notes

- Only one side of the paper was used so that notes could be cut up.
- Notes were colour coded according to source by drawing a continuous coloured line down the margin.
- Page numbers and any other ideas that came to mind were written in margins.
- The children kept a list of sources and their colour codes.

This meant that sources could easily be identified after notes had been cut up, for example, if the need arose to check information or add more detail.

When the information had been collected and recorded the process of organizing the notes began.

Organizing the notes

- All the notes were read through.
- Main ideas were identified, e.g. circus animals' 'living conditions', 'training', 'behaviour'.
- Notes were then cut up and placed in sets according to what main idea they supported.
- Each set was then read through and further subdivisions made, e.g. 'training' was subdivided into 'big cats' and 'elephants'.

Now that the content had been selected and the notes organized in various ways, the children could begin the process of composing the text.

Composing the text collaboratively

The children worked in pairs to compose sections of the text. They would have one of the subdivided sets of cut up notes (e.g. on the 'training of big cats') which they could physically rearrange. They had to organize the ideas and express them as clearly as possible for their intended audience.

This situation (which includes the above method of organizing notes) provides the flexible planning stage which is especially necessary in the case of non-narrative or non-chronological writing. Unlike narrative or story, which is organized on a chronological or 'what happened next' basis, there is no predetermined basis for organizing non-narrative writing. A logical way of ordering each

1 Fear and aggression

It is difficult to apply the term 'fear' to an animal without persuading the reader to compare it with the human experience of fear. This may be inaccurate because we do not know how human fear compares with that of an animal, neither do we know how fear affects different species. However, measurements of blood pressure and heart-rate, ear and tail movements, facial expressions, body postures and vocalisation provide a fairly accurate indication of the animal's experience.

What shows they are afraid?

In the circus ring, the big cats frequently display these signals very clearly. They will often respond to the trainer's commands by slinking across the ring, belly close to the ground, ears flattened, sometimes snarling loudly. A clear indication of fear.

1a Watch what lions and tigers do when the trainer tells them to do something.

If you go to a circus have a look to see if the lions and tigers are slinking across the ring, with their bellies close to the floor and their ears flattened. You may also hear them snarling loudly. This shows that they are afraid.

---

2 *Aggression is often the first response to fear, and a lion or tiger may be seen to paw threateningly at an outstretched whip.* An audience may well misinterpret these aggressive approaches, and marvel all the more at the trainer's daring.

Escape

Escape or flight behaviour is an important factor to consider when attempting to understand the training of circus animals. Biologically the significance of flight is obvious – protection from enemies. Virtually all animals have distinctive flight motivations which may be measured by a quantitative value – the flight distance. *If a potential enemy comes within the flight distance of an animal, it will attempt to flee. If confined and unable to retreat, the animal will cower, show 'fear' and issue a low intensity threat. If the intruder continues to approach, a critical distance will be reached, at which the insecure, apparently cowering animal will attack. Thus the lion tamer's 'skill' is largely based on the ability to assess this critical distance.*

2a When you see a lion or tiger wave its paw fiercely at its trainer's whip, this is often a sign that the animal is afraid.

The audience may think that it is very good and that the trainer is very daring.

If the trainer goes too close to the lions or tigers then they may be so scared that they try to escape. If they can't escape they may attack the trainer instead.

Figure 8.1   Showing how published texts were written in the children's own language
Items 1 and 2 are extracts from the RSPCA booklet *Animals in Circuses*
Items 1a and 2a show how Sue and Denise wrote sections of the RSPCA text in their own language

new text has to be worked out. This flexible situation also enables the teacher to help children when they need it – during the process of writing.

Apart from encouraging mutual support and awareness of audience, the collaborative work gave opportunity for:

- Organizing:

    Sue: What next / we've done this.
    Denise: We haven't done that one yet / I don't think / that's really the same as that one.

- Judging the effectiveness of the writing:

    Sue: You may also hear them snarling loudly.
    Denise: Growling loudly / roaring loudly.
    Sue: Snarling sounds better doesn't it / snaar . . . aagh . . .

- Experimenting with different forms of expression:

    Sue: . . . we can do like / *sometimes* the trainer does blah blah blah / and *other times* he does this / and sometimes he *even* / . . . chews tobacco.

- Developing the habit of casting back to get an overall sense of how the text is developing.

    Sue: . . . so let's just see if it goes with this . . . let's read it from the beginning.

Figure 8.1 shows two extracts from a published text (1 and 2) which can be compared with two samples of the children's writing (1a and 2a) to see what they wrote in their own language.

The zoo

The main source of information for this phase was a visit to a zoo.

Preparation for the visit

Lions, bears, elephants and chimpanzees had been focused on during the circus phase so these were also studied at the zoo. Each child was responsible for one animal in particular. Parts of *Understanding Zoo Animals* (Kidman Cox 1980) were read in order to help frame appropriate questions. The children also discussed what questions they would ask the education officer.

A visit to the zoo

The children collected and recorded information by:

- interviewing the education officer (the whole interview was tape recorded).
- observing the chosen animals and their living quarters and verbalizing those observations in order to tape record them (oral note taking).

- making rough sketches.
- taking photographs.

Using the information to compose a text

With the help of their tape-recorded information, their rough sketches and the teacher, the children made detailed drawings of the animal enclosures and wrote texts to complement the drawings which were labelled with numbers corresponding to the writing.

Some of the first attempts at writing were superficial. Even Amy was satisfied with a short list at first (Figure 8.2). The content in this case had not been collected and organized in writing as before and had to be built up through successive drafting. It was important to imagine what a reader might need or be interested to know. Amy and Sue quickly grasped the idea and were soon able to generate ideas with only a little prompting. The first drafts were done individually then they discussed them with each other and with the teacher.

Amy's second and third drafts are considerably expanded and provide examples of thinking on paper. In draft 2 (Figure 8.3) for example:

- She adds and changes words (lines 2, 4, and 24).
- She adds phrases and sentences using arrows and balloons (lines 8, 11 and 14).
- She changes numbers to reorganize the sequence.

In draft 3 (Figure 8.4) changes are still being made:

- The final sequence is established.
- She adds an introductory sentence.
- She adds information, e.g. 'This may sound cruel but . . .'.
- She sometimes inclines towards more impersonal writing, e.g. the language is changed from the active 'They have got lots of bushes . . .' (draft 2, lines 12 and 13) to the passive 'It is filled with bushes . . .' (draft 3)
- Punctuation and spelling are corrected.

Denise and Linda needed considerable prompting in order to make their work more explicit, elaborated and coherent.

It is very rewarding to support children in this way because the content and language is their own even if it has to be drawn from them. Denise's third draft (Figure 8.5) demonstrates how she often cut up her writing and used sellotape or paper clips to facilitate text organization.

Final phase: concluding and completing activities

This phase involved forming conclusions about zoos and circuses and dealing with the overall organization of the book. Some of the activities were as follows.

2 Caves.

1 Pool.

1 Ledge.

1 inside cage with dens inside.

Lots of bushes.

1 Tree with spikes to prevent lion ecscaping.

Figure 8.2 Amy's first attempt

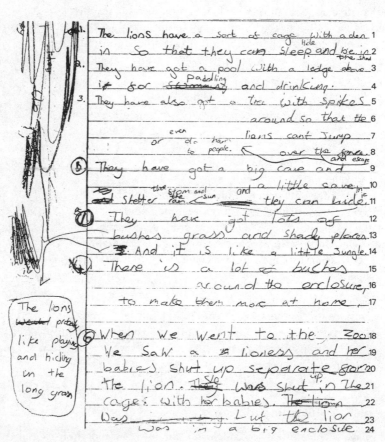

The lions have a sort of cage with a den 1
in so that they can sleep and be in 2
They have got a pool with a ledge above 3
it for paddling and drinking. 4
They have also got a tree with spikes 5
around so that the 6
even lions cant jump 7
or do harm to people. over the fence and escape 8
They have got a big cave and 9
shelter from rain and sun a little cave 10
they can hide. 11
They have got lots of 12
bushes grass and shady places. 13
And it is like a little jungle. 14
There is a lot of bushes 15
around the enclosure 16
to make them more at home. 17
When we went to the zoo 18
We saw a lioness and her 19
babies shut up separate from 20
the lion. was shut up in the 21
cage with her babies. 22
was but the lion 23
was in a big enclosure 24

The lions probably like playing and hiding in the long grass

Figure 8.3 Amy's second draft

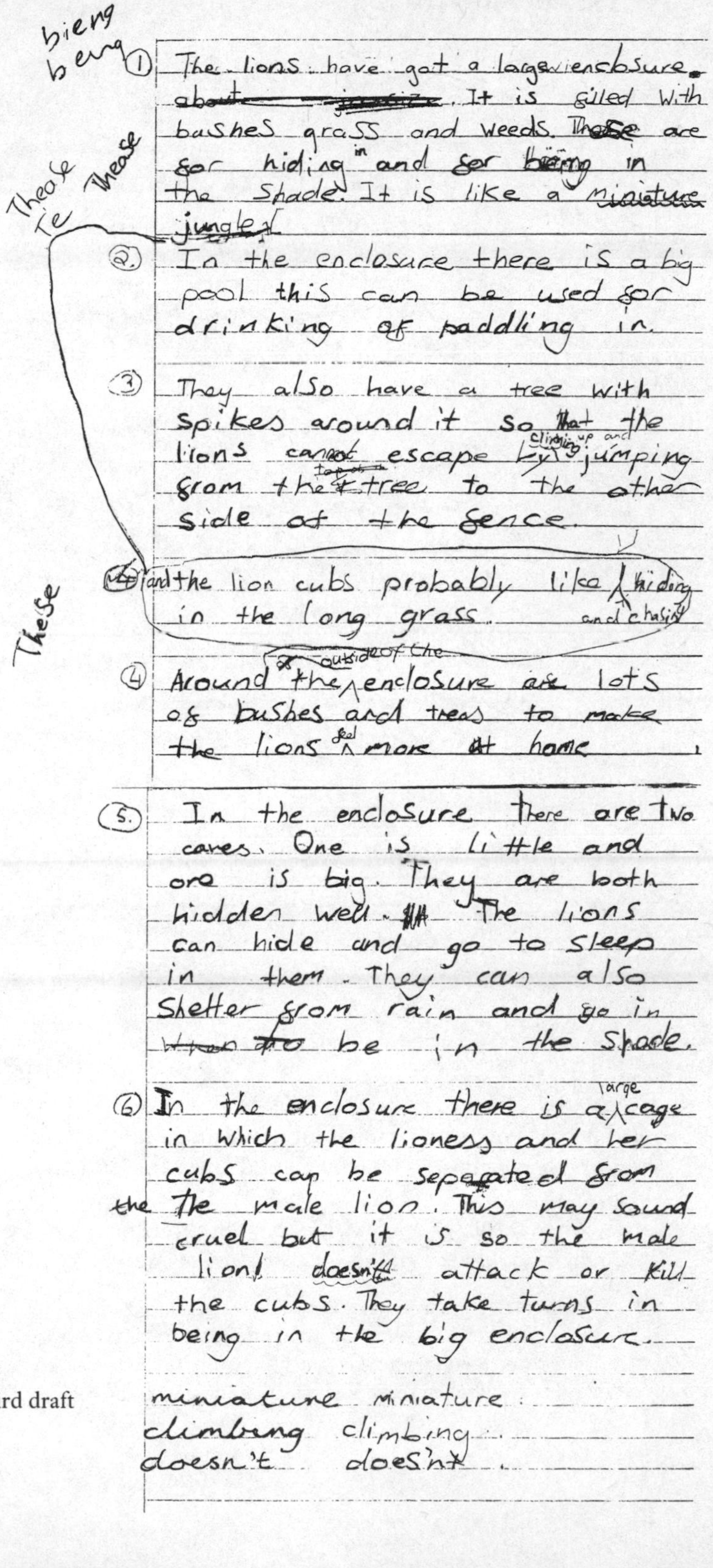

bieng
being

① The lions have got a large enclosure. ~~about~~ ~~justice~~ It is filled with bushes grass and weeds. These are for hiding in and for ~~bieng~~ in the shade. It is like a ~~miniature~~ jungle.

Those
Te Those

② In the enclosure there is a big pool this can be used for drinking of paddling in.

③ They also have a tree with spikes around it so that the lions ~~cannot~~ escape by ~~climbing up and~~ jumping from the ~~top tree~~ to the ~~other~~ side of the fence.

These

~~and the lion cubs probably like hiding in the long grass. and chasing~~

④ Around the ~~of outside of the~~ enclosure are lots of bushes and trees to make the lions feel more at home.

⑤ In the enclosure there are two caves. One is little and one is big. They are both hidden well. ~~###~~ The lions can hide and go to sleep in them. They can also shelter from rain and go in ~~when to~~ be in the shade.

⑥ In the enclosure there is a large cage in which the lioness and her cubs can be separated from the male lion. This may sound cruel but it is so the male lion doesn't attack or kill the cubs. They take turns in being in the big enclosure.

miniature   miniature
climbing   climbing
doesn't   doesn't

Figure 8.4 Amy's third draft

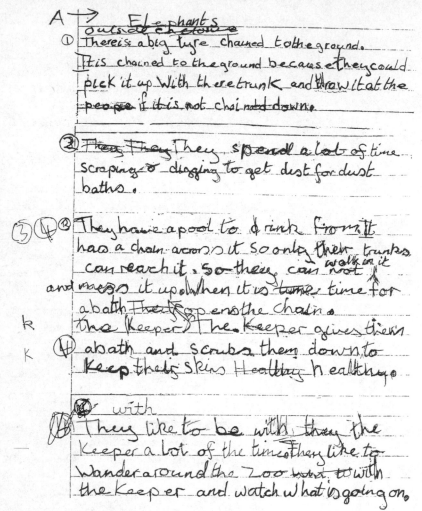

Figure 8.5 Part of Denise's third draft

Forming conclusions about zoos and circuses

There were opportunities for evaluating, judging, expressing opinions and forming conclusions both in talk and in writing, and for considering other points of view.

When the teacher asked how they felt about including the circus's point of view in their book, some of the children's replies were:

> I think it's good because you could . . . sort of put what they think . . . and then put what we think . . . put your own comments on what they said . . . underneath you could put what we think . . . then they (the readers) can know whether they would agree with the circus or whether they agree with the remarks that we say.

The children discussed what they thought of the circus's point of view and then wrote their views collaboratively:

> Circuses say that they give the animals exercise cages as well as their beast wagons. They also take some of the animals for walks, for example elephants and camels.
>
> But we think that even if circuses *do* give their animals exercise cages it still isn't enough, and they couldn't give the elephants and camels that much of a walk because we don't think they would be allowed to take them outside the circus grounds.

Here we can see the children's developing ability to present argument in writing. It is always helpful for children to have a written statement of the other side's point of view.

The girls discussed the question 'Do you think it is cruel to keep animals in zoos?' in order to sort out their ideas through talk. Later they made individual statements to be included in a section entitled 'What we think of zoos and circuses'. Amy, in some ways the most able writer, produced the following:

> I think that it is cruel to keep animals in zoos because they don't have the same surroundings and atmosphere as in the wild and they don't have enough things to do. In the zoo they have about the size of a classroom to live in, but in the wild they have as much space as they need.
>
> When we went to the zoo we met the education officer. He said that zoos were good because they stop the lions and the wild cats from eating the zebras and the small animals, but I think that it is natural for them to do it so it doesn't really matter.
>
> I think that circuses are much worse than zoos because they keep the animals in small beast wagons in the circus. But in the zoo the animals live in quite big enclosures, but they still aren't as good as the wild. The circus is worse than zoos because in circuses they use goads and they mainly train the animals, but in the zoo they don't train the animals or use any goads at all.
>
> But I'm not saying that zoos are good!

Linda, in some ways the least able, wrote:

> I think zoos are cruel because they keep their animals in cages – specially the owls. Owls like to fly around but they can't because they only have a small cage to fly in.
>
> Circuses are crueller than zoos because they keep the animals in beast wagons. The beast wagons are dark and the noise of the engines might frighten them.

Both of these are clearly expressed arguments written in an individual style.

Overall organization of the book

The various sections of the book were put together by clipping them to A4 size paper in a ring folder which allowed paragraphs, illustrations and pages to be rearranged. There was a lot of discussion about naming parts, chapters and sections. This involved the children in reading to ascertain 'What's it all about?'

This stage of the project provided further opportunities for learning about the aims, purposes and organization of information books:

- Their aims and purposes were made clear at the beginning of their book, for example, in a letter to the readers.
- They organized a line of subject development and provided some conclusions.
- They learned about:
  - logical arrangement
  - sequencing of facts
  - linking sections
  - contents
  - indexes
  - reference sections
  - suggestions for further activities

Conclusions

In addition to the experiences and learning opportunities already described, the children gained from:

- being given responsibility.
- learning to work collaboratively with others.
- a sense of achievement.
- self-concept enhancement (especially Denise and Linda).

Linda actually asked, very shyly but with obvious pride, 'Why was I chosen to write this book?'

Working in this collaborative way reveals what children are capable of. Clearly better results are facilitated by accustoming children to these methods of working and to this level of responsibility from an early age. Of course a project need not be so ambitious – the production of a simple information sheet, for example, would be easier to begin with.

Some very rewarding non-fiction book-writing activities may be undertaken with whole classes of very young children, say after visits to a farm or a zoo. The classes may be divided into small groups, each responsible for a particular chapter of the book, for example, 'Introduction', 'Cows', 'Pigs', 'Sheep', etc. and 'Ending'. Texts may be created in various ways:

- Through shared writing – small groups discuss and compose a chapter with their teacher who scribes for them on large paper on an easel (see McKenzie *et al.* 1985).
- Through tape-recorded discussion – small groups talk about a particular chapter both with and without their teacher. The teacher (or teacher and pupils) then uses the tape to write down the children's ideas using their own language.
- Through organizing non-narrative texts – small groups of children organize jumbled, cut-up sentences which they have composed themselves (e.g. about pigs) in order to create a logically ordered text.

The texts may be transcribed (by the teacher if necessary) into books with a list of contents and illustrated with children's drawings or photos. They may be photocopied and recordings made to support readers at listening centres.

Rudimentary research skills may be introduced when, for example, the teacher helps pupils to consult pictures or books in order to check the accuracy of their knowledge (teacher's and children's) or to discover new facts.

It is clear that there is great potential for developing reading abilities through the book writing activities described in this chapter. It should be emphasized that pupils were involved in realistic tasks: with real reasons for inquiry, real reasons for writing and real audiences in mind. In addition to creating non-fiction books in language that children can understand, the collaborative writing of information books provides a dynamic context for the organic growth of competencies in talking, listening and reading as well as writing. As Vygotsky (1983 p.268) says, 'What the child can do in co-operation today he can do alone tomorrow'.

Acknowledgements

I am grateful to Lewis Coley and Tracey Cameron of Moor Green Junior School, Birmingham, for their support. Particular thanks are due to a group of pupils for their bright ideas, unceasing industry and enthusiasm.

Thanks are also due to Barrie Wade for advice and help given during the book-writing experiment and in the writing of this chapter.

PART FIVE
Assessing and monitoring progress

9 Monitoring and assessing development

LYNDA YARD

Given the validity of a whole-language approach which integrates talking, listening, reading and writing, it is still possible for many teachers and parents to be uneasy about how progress is assessed. Some still hanker after a recording system as simple as 'Peter is on Book 2 and Jane is on Book 6', even though such information tells us nothing about the reading behaviour, interests or progress of either child. Others may still desperately seek for objective measurements such as reading ages even though these have long been discredited as reliable or valid measures of reading ability. The Bullock Report (1975), for example, pointed out that reading ages are usually derived from reading tests with words or sentences out of context and therefore measure only a fraction of the skills that a reader uses. Similarly the objective information that 'Peter has improved his reading age from 5.1 to 7.6 while Jane has improved from 9.1 to 11.6' seems to indicate that each child has made a similar rate of progress while, in fact, the books they have read, their attitudes to them, their needs, strengths and weaknesses might be radically different. At the other extreme some teachers have preferred simply to list the number of books a child has read. Again, however, 'Peter has read three books this week, while Jane has read eleven' may tell us next to nothing about development. Jane may have skim-read, her books may have been slighter than Peter's, she may have read without understanding, interest or enthusiasm. Clearly, whichever extreme we consider, reading is too complex an activity to assess by simplistic numerical means.

Barrie Wade (ed.)

One approach to assessment

Early chapters of this book have made clear how children begin to learn about reading and to develop as readers long before they come to school. They become aware that printed signs in the environment carry messages, they hear rhymes and jingles and enjoy patterns of repetition and, given the opportunity, they enjoy listening to and taking part in story telling and in the sharing of picture story books. Later chapters have shown how classroom reading experiences extend these early opportunities. Teachers tell stories from their own experience and retell well-known fairy tales and legends and invite children to tell and retell their own stories. Book corners look inviting and tempt children to browse and to share picture story-books and books made by children in the school. Stories with large print are shared and picture story-books and poems read and shared by the whole class several times a day. Notices around the classroom and school invite children to make meaning. Writing for real audiences makes the important link between writers and readers and develops understanding of how books are organized. This chapter considers ways of making sure that all the children in our classes are profiting fully from these experiences.

A group of teachers who were trying to build up a picture of each child's reading development, decided that a simple note of the title of a book shared by teacher and child would be an inadequate way of recording progress. Instead the group decided to make brief focused notes immediately after each weekly shared-reading session.

To give an actual example of our approach, the records made by Pauline Thomson of David, one child in her class of middle infants, follow. They were made quickly, immediately after sharing a story. It is important to remember that

Name: David

Date	Book	Child's strengths	Teacher strategies
17 Sept	*Smarty Pants*	He read it well, pointing as he read. He was proud of himself. Read with care.	I asked him to point.
25 Sept	*Smarty Pants*	He obviously enjoys this book. Read with care. He managed the rhymes, which meant reading ahead.	I looked at rhyming words with him.
5 Oct	*The Monster Book*	Retold in exact book language, pointing one-to-one as he read. When I referred him back, he could use previous chunks of reading to help him out.	Asked him to look back and find words he had read before.
19 Oct	*Smarty Pants*	Read really well; pointing with care. Remembered to include reading ahead to make words rhyme. Could point to 'Smarty Pants' and 'see me'.	Asked him to show me 'Smarty Pants' and the 'see me' all throughout book.

Figure 9.1 One child's progress

Date	Book	Child's strengths	Teacher strategies
21 Oct	*Cat on the Mat*	Fluent reading. Could point to all the words I asked him to.	Asked him to pick out some repeated words.
2 Nov	*Grandpa Grandpa*	Read well, decoding using small sight vocabulary and memorization.	
9 Nov	*Grandpa Grandpa*	Took his time, determined to read it correctly. Memorization helped.	I helped when he was stuck.
16 Nov	*The Monster's Party*	Very confident, managed to pick out 'monster' 'fly' and 'can' with no help. Self-correcting now.	Asked him for some words.
23 Nov	*The Red Rose*	Persisted well, determined to read it correctly. Pointed one-to-one. Memorization, but some use of context cues.	I helped him to refer back.
30 Nov	*The Monster's Party*	Super, fluent confident reading. Read with assurance. Likes story because of the monster and also because he had his birthday party on Saturday.	Asked him why he likes this book. I enjoyed it.
11 Dec	*The Monster's Party*	Read well, pointing as he read. Could tell me he knew the word 'dance' because it began with a 'd'.	Asked him to point. Asked him to show me 'monster'.

Figure 9.2   Recording David's progress

the notes do not describe all David's reading. During the year he would have experienced many more stories at home and at school. The record simply describes those he chose to share on an individual basis with his teacher. In order to keep records focused, we decided we would concentrate on just two features of the shared reading sessions: the child's strengths, the things the teacher noticed the child had coped with well and the teacher strategies, the ways in which we helped during the session.

At the beginning of the year the books David chose to share were ones he knew well, with lots of rhyme and repetition; he chose one three times as he gradually gained in confidence. The section 'Teacher strategies' gives some indication of help given; David was invited to point below the print as he retold the story from

Date	Book	Child's strengths	Teacher strategies
5 Jan	Dear Zoo	Read well, after initial anxiety. He thought he could remember it, but his memorization wasn't as strong as he hoped. He wanted to give up, but with support and using his decoding skills, he managed well.	Supported him during his reading of the text. Encouraged him to have a go.
25 Jan	Grandpa Grandpa	Read well. He could pick out any words I asked him using initial letter clues.	Asked him to pick out some words.
24 Feb	Dear Zoo	Good fluent reading of a known text.	
29 Feb	The Rabbit's Wedding	Read first five pages of text, managing well, using context and initial letter clues.	Prompted him when needed to keep flow.
1 Mar	The Rabbit's Wedding	We carried on to middle page. He is beginning to decode very well.	I enjoyed it!
3 Mar	The Rabbit's Wedding	Read it all! Great stuff.	

Figure 9.3 David's further progress

memory, encouraged to use rhyming words and helped to begin to build up a small sight vocabulary.

Gradually David increased the number of books he chose to share, though he still chose books from the same series, ones he would have known well from group reading sessions. The teacher helped by encouraging him to make use of his increasing sight vocabulary, by giving him time to be independent and by

Date	Book	Child's strengths	Teacher strategies
9 Mar	Clean Enough	He read well. He is taking on a bit more each time. Recognized lots of words.	I helped when he was stuck.
17 Mar	Dear Zoo	Good word attack. Not afraid of words.	
24 Mar	Sing a Song	Enjoyed reading this known text.	I enjoyed it too!

Date	Book	Child's strengths	Teacher strategies
19 Apl	*Karen at the Zoo*	He had read half of this to Mrs B. He carried on, using his sight vocab. to take him through the text. Enjoying himself.	Encouraged him to finish off reading it with another child.
26 Apl	*Where's Spot?*	He obviously enjoyed reading it. Read rather than retold the story. Looked carefully at words and decoded well, using initial letters, context and memorization.	I enjoyed it! I do like Spot.
3 May	*The Loose Tooth*	A confident assured read. Really super stuff. His reading had a fluency it hasn't had before.	I enjoyed it.
5 May	*The Loose Tooth*	A good choice of book – the natural flow of text aided reading. He can read it again today to Mrs B. who is sure to be impressed.	Gave him time to predict words in context. Lots of praise. Suggested he read it to Mrs B.
9 May	*Buttons and Bows*	An assured and confident read. He kept the flow going, reread to self-correct. Super!	He had shared it with Mrs B.
24 May	*Rally Car* (Own book, written at home)	He has recently got into writing, and made this book at home with his dad.	We talked about how he set about this piece of writing. Gave lots of praise.
7 June	*Ten go Hopping*	A super read. Very keen to get it right. Decoding well.	I really praised him.
14 June	*In Bed*	He likes these little books. He's taking on more and more unknown texts and handling them well.	
5 July	*Duck in the Box*	He is so proud of himself and his ability to handle a text all on his own.	Needed very little help.
17 July	*The Old Plane* (his own story)	Fluent read. Very proud of being an author. Read his book to Mrs G. and Mr I.	Asked him to share it with other members of staff.

Figure 9.4   David is becoming a fluent reader

sharing his enjoyment. She noticed that he began to make use of initial letter clues.

David's confidence increased and he extended the range of books he chose to share. Encouraged by his teacher, he made use of his sight vocabulary, initial letter clues, and the sense of the story to make meaning. The teacher's enthusiasm and encouragement is evident.

David's choice of stories became more varied as his own belief in his ability increased. The teacher helped by praise and by encouraging him to read to other children and adults in the school.

These brief notes show a part of one child's journey during one school year. All children develop as readers in different ways. By making brief notes like these, we can chart each journey, and be clear about appropriate ways of helping each child.

A developmental record of emergent reading

Teachers who were recording reading development in this way began to notice that, although no two children developed in exactly the same way, some developmental stages were common to many children. We wondered if we could present these observations in a way that would be helpful to us and to other teachers. The document we produced, 'A developmental record of emergent reading' (Figure 9.5), is the result of many meetings and much discussion and redrafting over an initial period of two terms and during a pilot year involving 75 teachers using the record alongside the weekly records of 2,400 children like David. We now feel confident that it is a useful resource for individual teachers and for a whole school policy of assessing reading development.

Used as a resource for individual teachers, the developmental record gives some indication of the most common developmental stages in the early years of reading. After three years of monitoring reading development in this way we have yet to find any two children whose reading follows exactly the same pattern and we have noticed that many children omit some stages. The developmental record is arranged with stages representing attitude to reading on one side and those about print awareness on the other. We must emphasize that both sets of behaviour are of equal importance; neither takes priority.

The developmental record gives teachers a possible indication of developmental stages. Teachers who have used the record in the pilot year were asked to comment on its effectiveness and the following responses are typical:

'I found that children do go through stages indicated on the record, exciting to see them do this.'

'As a teacher new to this approach to reading, the guidelines were good to refer to.'

'Useful to be aware of stages child might pass through.'

'Became part of my recording language.'

'At the end of the year you have a complete record of the child's reading progress.'

The teacher who made the last comment was clearly using the developmental record as a checklist for assessment of progress as well as a guideline for development. Used in this way, at regular intervals, information can be transferred from the weekly records (child's strengths, teacher's strategies) to the developmental record.

Information is transferred by the teacher putting a diagonal line across the appropriate rectangle when the behaviour is first noticed and by recrossing in the opposite direction when the stage is an integral part of the child's reading behaviour.

Some schools decided to use a different coloured pen for each year of the child's school life so that the pattern of development could be clearly seen. Teachers have files with individual weekly records followed by the developmental record for each child. At the end of the academic year this complete file is handed to the next teacher. At any time of the year the teacher can give a helpful snap-shot assessment of reading development for each child in the class.

There are problems, some of which were raised during the first year of trial:

'I think it ought to be started from Reception, it doesn't make sense to start it later.'

'We must remember to explain to new members of staff that the record is not a set progression.'

'Not extensive enough for able readers.'

Phased introduction starting in the reception year is probably the easiest way of using the developmental record. Schools who have introduced it in all three years of the infant school decided to record the development only during that specific academic year, as it seemed inappropriate to invent early stages. An indication of the year in which the record is first used is probably helpful in this instance. Continual school-based and LEA in-service training of new members of staff is as necessary for this approach, as for any other curriculum innovation.

Later stages of reading development

We expected that the developmental record would be useful for all three years of the infant school. In practice many children read independently before junior school transfer and the record does not monitor the continued development of more experienced readers. Recently groups of teachers from the infant and junior stages have produced a document indicating stages of reading development in the primary years. Once again, this document is the result of many meetings and much discussion. In a fourth draft stage it is now being piloted by volunteer infant, junior and primary schools. We hope that in its final draft it will be a useful resource for teachers of children reading for real in the primary stages and a useful resource for whole school record keeping and assessment of reading development. Figure 9.6 therefore represents our thinking so far, before final modifications.

Figure 9.5   A developmental record of emergent reading

This record sheet is intended to be used simply as a guide. We emphasize that we believe emergent reading follows no linear progression and that the sequence of development is unique for each child.

ATTITUDE TO READING			
Observes shared reading	Sharing 1 to 1 willing to hold book	Sharing 1 to 1 comments on picture/story details	Relates own experience listening 1 to 1
Sharing 1 to 1 willing to tell story first to adult	Concentrates and enjoys a story in a group	Concentrates and enjoys a story read to class	Chooses to share a book with an adult
Enjoys illustrations as an integral part of the story	Mulls over picture details	Chooses to browse through books alone	Handles books with care

Keeps returning to special books he/she can really read	Looks for books by favourite authors	Discusses story in detail	Looks for favourite sets of books	Returns to favourite books	Enjoys sharing a story aloud with friends

Willing to tackle an unseen text	Eager to read part of a new story to others	Enjoys reading known texts aloud with expression	Browses with friends –shared enjoyment	Enjoys reading silently

PRINT AWARENESS

Aware of some public print

INCREASING PRINT AWARENESS

Aware of initial letter of own name	Recognizes own name	Notices print around classroom

SHARING 1 to 1

...turns pages accurately with help to find beginning	...turns pages accurately	...predicts during first reading	...joins in repeated sections	...echoes adult reading

RE-TELLING A STORY

Turns pages randomly commenting on pictures	Consistently looks at left hand page first	...Relates it to own experiences	...with accurate page turning commenting on some pictures	...with accurate page turning, inventing own story

INCREASING PRINT AWARENESS

Looks for words beginning with initial letter of own name	Recognizes names of some of friends	Identifies some print in the classroom	Some sight vocabulary of high interest words

RE-TELLING A STORY

...uses picture clues	...in own words sequence correct	...in own words and some book language	...accurately from memory	...accurately pointing towards but not focusing on print	Is able to focus on print
...finger scanning direction correct but not focusing on print	...finger scanning matches first and last word, one line phrase	...finger scanning left → right left → right correct	...memorises simple text and matches words 1 to 1	...known text matches words making contextually correct guesses	Place: holds with finger

INCREASING PRINT AWARENESS

Emphasizes changes of type in the print	Begins to notice words that are the same	Begins to notice punctuation	Aware of some initial sounds	Knows names of some letters	Known text uses initial letter clues
Realizes when comes across unknown words	Self-corrects using initial letter clues	Self-corrects by re-reading part of phrase or sentence	Some sight vocabulary	Notices patterns within words	Aware of some phonic clusters

BEGINNING OF INDEPENDENCE

Takes over from adult on initial reading of text	Able to tackle unknown text

If the document is used as a development record we suggest that a diagonal line is made across the specific rectangle when the behaviour is first noticed and a further line added in the opposite direction when the behaviour is a definite part of the child's development. We suggest the use of pens of three different colours, for example; red for reception, green for middle and blue for the top year.

Figure 9.6 Developmental record for reading in the primary years

> The sequence of development is unique for each child

Chooses to read	ATTITUDE TO READING		Aims to read completely independently
	Looks for favourite 'sets' and authors	Re-reads favourite stories	
Responds to the rhythm, patterns of language	Responds to notices in the classroom and school	Seeks specific stories	Chooses to read information books for pleasure
Chooses to read a wide variety of fiction	Enjoys reading plays	Enjoys reading aloud	Responds to the rhythm/ language of poetry
	Enjoys reading silently	Enjoys reading stories with friends	

Keen to predict and reflect while reading	INVOLVEMENT WITH BOOKS		Appreciates the styles of different illustrators
Empathizes with main characters	Perceived the 'hidden' text	While reading relates to own experiences and other books	Skims books first when making a choice
Developing critical response	Sustains interest in long stories– serial stories in chapters	Perseveres to 'get into' books of different styles	Building experiences gained from literature into own life

BEGINNING OF INDEPENDENCE	
Takes over from adult on initial reading of text	Able to tackle unknown text

DEVELOPING READING COMPETENCE			
Makes increasing use of print	Uses initial letter cues and aware of word endings	Unknown words – reads ahead, then goes back	Consistently uses a variety of cues
Useful sight vocabulary	Able to reflect and predict while reading	Able to choose books appropriate for reading ability	Able to read new texts after sharing first few pages
Desire to read completely accurately	Able to read independently	Able to read a story accurately having first browsed independently	Able to read an 'unknown' story
Able to read silently	Abe to summarize stories concisely and coherently	Able, using pictures,cover and 'blurb' to make appropriate predictions about a story	Responds to print conventions

READING FOR INFORMATION		
Able to use an index	Able to use a contents table	Uses appropriate reference materials
Able to skim for general information	Able to scan and extract specific information	Able to summarize information

Maths worksheets	Instructions for games	ABLE TO READ, UNDERSTAND, AND EXTRACT INFORMATION FROM A VARIETY OF SOURCES		Posters	Weather reports
Science experiments	Recipes			News-papers	TV prog-rammes
Dictionaries	Computer programs	Library catalogues		Catalogues	Time-tables
Thesaurus	Encyclopaedias	Reference books		Advert-isements	Charts

If the document is used as a developmental record we suggest that a diagonal line is made across the specific rectangle when the behaviour is first noticed and a further line added in the opposite direction when the behaviour is a definite part of the child's development. We suggest pens of different colours are used for each year of school.

The format is similar to that of the earlier developmental record; it does not replace detailed observations made when teacher and child share stories, but again can be used as guidelines or a checklist in conjunction with weekly records. As the child increases in confidence and competence as a reader in the primary years the conference between teacher and child develops. Many teachers encourage children to keep logs or records noting books they have really enjoyed and sections of stories that they would like to share and discuss with their teacher. We need to be familiar with all the stories being read by children, so we can discuss with individuals, assess their involvement and make recommendations and suggestions for further reading. This represents a lot of teacher time spent reading, but it is time well spent if only to give us insights into the lives and feelings of the children we teach. What better time to read children's stories than in quiet reading sessions when everyone, including the teacher, reads books of their own choice, and what better teacher than Ramona on the real joy of these sessions?

> How peaceful it was to be left alone in school. She could read without trying to hide her book under the desk or behind a bigger book. She was not expected to write lists of words she did not know, so she could figure them out by skipping and guessing. Mrs Whaley did not expect the class to write summaries of what they read either, so she did not have to choose easy books to make sure she would get her summary right. Now if Mrs Whaley would leave her alone to draw, too, school would be almost perfect.
>   Yes, Sustained Silent Reading was the best part of the day.
>   *Ramona Quimby Age 8*, Beverly Cleary

Our aim is to help children to develop as committed, competent and avid readers, and for them to retain the joy of reading throughout the primary years and on to the secondary school. The structure of recording reading development described enables us to make insightful decisions about the most appropriate ways of helping each child. No child is left to flounder. Useful strategies employed are praised and reinforced by the teacher, and sound judgements made of times when it is most valuable to the child for us to intervene.

Acknowledgements

Thanks are due to teachers in Croydon, who have spent so much of their time analysing children's reading development and to the many children we have monitored who have given us insights into reading development.

Lynda Yard is an advisory teacher in the London Borough of Croydon. The views expressed are not necessarily a statement of the official policy of the London Borough of Croydon.

Books referred to in this chapter

Ramona Quimby Age 8, Beverly Cleary, Puffin
Smarty Pants, S. Berry, Arnold Wheaton, *Story Chest*

Grandpa, Grandpa, S. Berry, Arnold Wheaton, *Story Chest*
The Red Rose, Arnold Wheaton, *Story Chest*
Sing a Story, S. Berry, Arnold Wheaton, *Story Chest*
The Monster's Party, Arnold Wheaton, *Story Chest*
Cat on the Mat, Brian Wildsmith, Oxford University Press
Dear Zoo, Rod Campbell, Puffin
The Rabbit's Wedding, Garth Williams, Collins (Armanda)
Clean Enough, Kevin Henkes, Kestrel
Karen at the Zoo, Jessie Reid, Link Up
Where's Spot?, Eric Hill, Heinemann
The Loose Tooth, David Mackay, Longman (Breakthrough)
Buttons and Bows, Frances Knowles, Longman (Breakthrough)
Ten Go Hopping, Viv Allbright, Faber
In Bed, Brian Thompson, Longman (Breakthrough)
Duck in the Box, Paul Groves, Longman

10 Learning to read – a two-year study of beginner readers

MURIEL BRIDGE

'How *do* young children learn to read?'

Teachers have long been teased by this bristling question. In an attempt to shed perhaps more light than heat on an area notorious for contention and swings of fashion, the Leicestershire Literacy Support Service (LLSS) undertook a literacy initiative and evaluation study between 1986 and 1988.

It grew from twin roots – from years of experience with older children (who had found it profoundly difficult to learn to read) and from a lively awareness of the stimulating whole-language ideas emerging during the 1970s and 1980s. Following the encouraging and positive responses to a whole language approach by these older pupils, the inevitable question arose, 'If whole language helps "failed" readers, why not pre-empt failure for beginner readers?' So a literacy initiative, known affectionately as LITINIT, was planned.

The initiative

The theory and practice of whole-language (WL) teaching (first known locally as 'story method' and later as 'story approach') was canvassed through seminars for all headteachers of primary age pupils, including some from special schools. Talks, backed up by a home-made video film and a purpose-written book, *Once Upon a Time . . .* , provoked thoughtful and widespread discussion; key texts such as Bennett, Holdaway, Smith and Waterland were made available for purchase as staffroom resources. Head-teachers were asked to consider whether their schools would like to take part in an evaluation study. When volunteers were later called for, 58 schools responded. Class teachers were inducted at the end of the term preceding the study and supported throughout; a random sample of pupils was selected from a random sample of schools.

Aims of the study

The evaluation study set out to compare two school populations of five-year-old pupils, one using traditional methods and the other a whole language approach to learning to read.

'Traditional' (T) is a label indicating the teacher's use of graded reading schemes based on the expectation that pupils will progress by a series of clearly delineated steps. First, sight words are taught using flash cards; letter sounds and word building follow; the child decodes text from these small elements, eventually reaching the stage of comprehension. The entire hierarchical process is teacher controlled and children are expected to fit the system.

'Whole language', in contrast, is a term signalling pupil-controlled, developmental learning. Pupils are immersed naturally in literacy experiences throughout the day. Each child may choose freely at any time from a variety of books written by story-telling authors. Their experience of sharing the story – listening while it is read to them, 'following' the text, enjoying the pictures – dynamically engages their whole personality. They find the story experience so deeply satisfying that they want to re-live it, many times! At first they reconstruct the text prompted by the pictures. (With a new story as yet unheard, they ad lib to the pictures.) Gradually they become more fastidious in matching their utterances to the words on the page. From such cumulative experiences they derive the necessary technical skills for independence (such skills as identifying particular words and letters, using cues and strategies efficiently, responding to punctuation). The meaning-making process is aided by teachers who ensure that the skills *do* develop out of the enriching whole story experience.

In the evaluation study, children's developing reading behaviours were observed in terms of their attitude to books, stories and reading and their ability to respond to text, assessed by both quantitative and qualitative measures.

Measuring progress

But measuring the development of such reading behaviours posed a considerable challenge! Clearly, more was involved than 'counting words' or administering standardized tests.

For the first year, information was gathered from three sources:

- detailed, open-ended logs kept throughout the year by the supporting LLSS teachers.
- questionnaire-based interviews at the end of the year with pupils' teachers.
- pupil interviews at the beginning and end of the year, tape-recorded for later analysis.

While the 20-minute pupil interviews were meticulously structured, they were kept as relaxed and natural as possible in a quiet, familiar setting. Pupil and assessor talked about 'favourite things' to tap attitudes to books, stories and reading. Next, a nursery rhyme book was shared to assess book-handling skills and the child's ability to make a voice–print match. Then a reading scheme book was used briefly to sample knowledge of book terms. But the focal interview point was the sharing of a real but simply told story (*The Boy and his Mother*, Warne). A priming discussion explored the storyline via the title and pictures. The assessor then read part of the story with occasional pregnant pauses at strategic words and phrases which would reveal the child's use of available cues. Lastly, the child made a solo attempt at the concluding three pages (38 words), supported by prompts as necessary. The final element of a graded word reading test (Burt, 1972 norms) was included to satisfy the need for a standardized instrument; it was one which would present a deliberately 'hard' test!

At the end of the second year, and in the light of first-year experiences, more sensitive measures were devised. Attitudes were sampled by two pupil question-naires, 'Reading at home' and 'At school', containing 16 questions in all. Reading behaviours were observed in an extended shared-story session. For this, a story was written for the textless Ginn Little Book, *Have You Seen my Shoe?* The story language was carefully 'graded' so that the first few pages required the children to use picture cues together with their memory for phrases they had heard in the priming session. Gradually the integrated use of more cues and strategies was required, the final page making quite sophisticated demands. The unique text, with a reading level range of something like 5+ to 8+ years, had the advantage of being new to every pupil.

They were told that the reason for sharing this draft story was to help the author get it 'just right' for children of their age. From the twelve pages of text, pupils were asked to read parts of four pages – a total of 196 running words. Further marks were allocated for 'expression'. As before, interviews were tape-recorded and later evaluated. The shared story proved a highly satisfactory instrument for scrutinizing 20 aspects of reading behaviour. The Burt graded word reading test was again included.

Results

After the first year

At the end of the first year, 1986–87, while no statistically significant differences between the two samples emerged, a number of important qualitative differences were observed. For the traditional sample, the status quo with reading methods meant that the expectations, attitudes and relationships of children, parents and teachers, as well as pupil progress, remained stable. However, it was noted that some parents were in fact using a whole-language approach quite naturally at home.

For the whole-language sample it was noticeable that:

• Pupils chose to read and reread more books more often, with a greater depth of involvement in the story.

- All children, *including the weakest*, sustained exceptional enthusiasm for learning to read, for books and stories.
- All pupils showed confidence in themselves as readers, even the 'slow starters'.
- Pupils gained an earlier understanding of the purposes of reading and a broader understanding of the processes involved.
- Pupils showed increasing critical awareness and appreciation of books, authors and illustrators.
- Pupils' reading aloud tended to be expressive from the beginning.
- A WL approach appeared to encourage generalized development across a broad front, including:

  – language use, especially the oracy of pupils from deprived backgrounds;
  – social aspects – more frequent and more positive book-mediated contacts were made between pupils, between pupils and their teachers and between pupils and their parents;
  – curriculum participation: pupils tended to take a fuller and more confident part in other areas of the curriculum; in particular, the content and quality of spoken and written language were enhanced together with sharpened observation skills.

- While pupils were slower to establish a sight vocabulary, often seeming to be at a standstill for a nerve-racking period, a sudden breakthrough point was reached after which progress accelerated.
- A WL approach compelled teachers to make innovations and to gain insights into the reading process.
- WL offered opportunities in the routine extended 'reading interviews' for teachers to develop a deeper understanding of and closer ties with each pupil.
- Teachers commented on the improved quantity and quality of home–school liaison.

WL teachers expressed particular concern about the very real stress they experienced in piloting a 'new' approach, involving as it did extra record keeping, considerably more demands from children to share books, while battling with their own uncertainties and those of some parents in the early stages. Assessors were impressed by the strikingly dynamic quality of learning in the WL classrooms.

After the second year

At the end of the second year, 1987–88, not only were the differences in learning quality maintained, but significant statistical differences between the two samples were evident. WL pupils showed significant gains in attitude and in reading behaviours although not in reading age gains. The 24 aspects of reading behaviour which were studied are shown in Figure 10.1, with statistical results tabulated in Figure 10.2. (The term 'cues' is used as a convenient shorthand for 'cues and strategies'.)

1	Attitude	13	Cues + HT (uses heard text)
2	Reading behaviours	14	MW (misses a word)
3	Expression	15	PS (page/wider search)
4	Variety of positive cues (cues +)	16	Cues − FF (false fluency)
5	Variety of negative cues (cues −)	17	AN (accepts nonsense)
6	Cues + C (self-correction)	18	IC (inappropriate cue)
7	RA (reads ahead)	19	W (waits)
8	CB (checks back)	20	[ ] (omits)
9	PhI (uses initial phonics)	21	BURT n/o words year 2
10	PhS (sounds out – phonics)	22	BURT n/o words years 1 + 2
11	P (uses picture cues)	23	BURT r.a. year 2
12	Pr (uses priming)	24	BURT r.a. years 1 + 2

Figure 10.1   The 24 aspects of reading behaviour

Significant statistical differences were obtained in 17 of the 24 items. The 7 items which did not reach a level of statistical significance were:

- sounding out words (PhS, a positive cue) (Almost equal use by both samples).
- use of priming (Pr, a positive cue) } (The T sample took advantage of these unaccustomed procedures).
- use of 'heard Text' (HT, a positive cue).
- the four BURT results (n/o new words recognized in year 2, also expressed as reading age; n/o words recognized over whole period, also r.a.).

WL pupils achieved significantly higher scores than T pupils in their

- attitude to books, stories and themselves as readers
- expression when reading aloud
- variety of positive reading cues used
- self-correction strategies
- reading ahead strategies
- initial phonic cue usage
- picture cue usage
- word omission by design
- page (or wider textual) search for cues

WL pupils achieved significantly lower scores in their use of:

- a variety of negative cues
- false fluency i.e. keeping vocal flow regardless of sense
- accepting a nonsense reading
- word omission by default

In addition, WL pupils achieved higher scores in their

- general reading behaviours as evaluated by a running record (196 words)
- use of checking back in the text for cues (a positive strategy)

	Whole language			Traditional			
	Total	Mean	SD	Total	Mean	SD	Significance
ATTITUDE	1077	31.68	5.51	933	27.44	6.07	2.97*
READING BEHAV.S	5648	166.11	40.89	4916	144.59	44.63	2.04+
EXPRESSN.	98	2.88	0.99	44	1.29	1.52	5.04*
VARIETY CUES +	280	8.23	2.01	186	5.47	2.44	5.01*
VARIETY CUES −	26	0.76	0.94	75	2.20	1.32	−5.10*
CUES + C	32	0.94	0.23	20	0.59	0.49	3.71*
CUES + RA	28	0.82	0.38	8	0.23	0.42	5.98*
CUES + CB	23	0.68	0.47	14	0.41	0.49	2.28+
CUES + PhI	34	1.00	0.00	27	0.79	0.40	3.01*
CUES + PhS	24	0.70	0.45	23	0.68	0.47	0.18
CUES + P	34	1.00	0.00	17	0.50	0.50	5.74*
CUES + Pr	34	1.00	0.00	32	0.94	0.23	1.50
CUES + HT	34	1.00	0.00	31	0.91	0.28	1.85
CUES + MW	18	0.53	0.50	7	0.21	0.40	2.87*
CUES + PS	19	0.56	0.50	7	0.21	0.40	3.14*
CUES − FF	0	0.00	0.00	7	0.21	0.40	−3.02*
CUES − AN	3	0.09	0.28	18	0.53	0.50	−4.41*
CUES − IC	0	0.00	0.00	5	0.15	0.35	−2.46+
CUES − W	15	0.44	0.50	24	0.71	0.46	−2.25+
CUES − [ ]	8	0.23	0.42	21	0.62	0.49	−3.47*
BURT GAINS n/o W (2)	492	14.47	6.60	484	14.23	7.96	0.13
BURT GAINS n/o W (1+2)	941	27.68	13.01	888	26.12	12.11	0.50
BURT GAINS r.a. (2)	444	13.06	6.27	445	13.09	7.75	−0.01
BURT GAINS r.a. (1+2)	827	24.32	12.13	757	22.26	11.24	0.72

* Denotes significant at 1 per cent level
+ Denotes significant at 5 per cent level

Figure 10.2 Scoring 24 aspects of reading behaviour

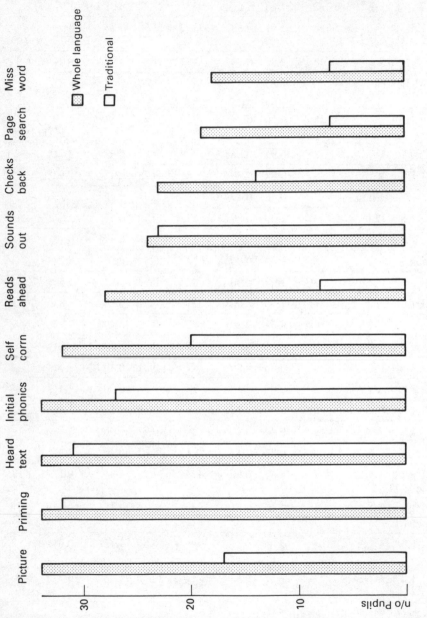

Figure 10.3   Using positive cues

- failure to choose inappropriate cues
- reliance on waiting for a prompt

'Top-' and 'bottom-' gaining pupils

After two years, all 'top-' and 'bottom-' gaining pupils maintained their relative positions as far as the Burt test and reading behaviour gains were concerned. However, the weakest WL pupils continued to register an average attitude score which was, in fact, higher than the average T attitude score and considerably higher than the 'bottom' T pupils' scores. The same pattern of response applied to pupils' use of expression, use of positive cues and strategies and use of negative cues and strategies. Figures 10.3–10.5 highlight interesting differences in cue usage by WL and T pupils. Figure 10.3 shows the greater overall use of cues and strategies made by WL pupils, all using the four key early reading cues of pictures, priming, heard text and initial phonics. Surprising is the failure of almost half the T pupils to use picture cues at all! Other graphically striking contrasts between the two samples are their use of self-correction, reading ahead, page search and deliberate word omission strategies.

Figure 10.4(a) illustrates the same cue usage but in rank order of use. The T sample's eager use of two cues not normally afforded them in traditional teaching – priming and heard text – demonstrates how essential these props are in the early months before independence to promote confidence, understanding and a fluent speed.

Figure 10.4(b) displays rank order of negative cue usage. False fluency and inappropriate cues were not used by WL pupils at all. Waiting indicates a helpless dependence on prompts where a pupil's repertoire of positive cues and strategies is impoverished. Not only did more T pupils than WL pupils rely on teacher-prompts, but their reliance was more frequent. The average 'take up' of potential positive cues by WL pupils was 80 per cent, while the average 'take up' of potential positive cues by T pupils was 52 per cent. The average 'take up' of potential negative cues by WL pupils was 13.5 per cent but the average 'take-up' of potential negative cues by T pupils was 41 per cent.

Discussion

There is no indication that children reared on a whole-language diet will learn to read any faster than children taught by traditional methods. Indeed, the slow take off of WL pupils caused their teachers considerable trauma! Is it possible that such a learning pace should be considered normal, while underlying reading behaviours are developing and integrating? Is the progress usually associated with traditional teaching in fact a forced, hot-house effect which does not correspond to a natural learning rate?

Certainly, the WL pupils were not disadvantaged in the long run. The most striking differences between the two groups show the WL pupils advantaged by their:

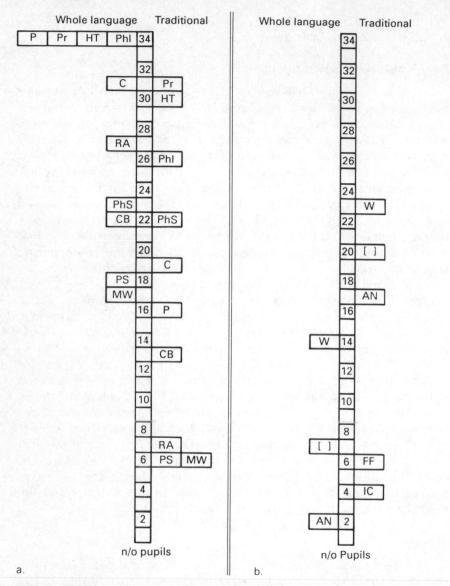

Figures 10.4(a) Popularity ranking of positive cues and **(b)** popularity ranking of negative cues.

- more positive attitude shown in
  - greater membership of public libraries;
  - greater voluntary use of books, shown in frequency of sharing books with other than teacher, in sharing books more often at home and in bringing more books from home to share in school;

- more positive self-image as readers.
- superior storying abilities.
- greater use of expression when reading aloud.
- wider use of positive reading cues and strategies.
- negligible use of inappropriate or negative reading cues and strategies.

With little variation, the more precocious and the less mature pupils retained their positions as 'top-' and 'bottom-' gaining pupils after two years. The most noticeable feature, however, was the higher morale of poor WL pupils who continued to enjoy stories and largely maintain a healthy self-image; who used greater expression when reading and who employed a wide variety of cues and strategies, as yet immature.

Most reading behaviours of WL pupils after two years are demonstrably more mature and independent than those of traditionally taught pupils. What value, then, should be attached to measuring progress by standardized graded word tests, since all the behaviours noted above are 'hidden' beneath what appear to be similar standardized scores? Are not later reading habits and competences likely to be more positive and effective

- when children show at an early age a marked priority for and pleasure in sharing books?
- when children make a search for meaning their first objective?
- when children begin to develop a strategically integrated use of many positive reading cues?

Such early reading behaviours must surely give children a greater freedom and independence as readers who will be prepared not only to adapt their styles of reading to suit the text in hand, but who will always be ready to engage with and consult books as a first friendly source of expertise and pleasure.

After two years, there are indications that a whole-language approach may convince more young learners of the long-term value of reading and books. We need to observe the same pupils in ten years time to discover if that is the case.

Acknowledgements

My grateful thanks are due to Angela White (Head of Leicestershire Literacy Support Service) for her generous encouragement and support throughout the Project and to the Leicestershire Education Authority for permission to use the findings in this chapter.

References

Arnold, H. (1982). *Listening to Children Reading*, London, Hodder and Stoughton.

Bardgett, K. (1977). 'The nature of reluctance', in J. L. Foster (ed.), *Reluctant to Read*, London, Ward Lock Education.

Barnes, D., Britton, J. N. and Rosen, H. (1969). *Language, Learner and the School*, Harmondsworth, Penguin Education.

Bennett, J. (1979). *Learning to Read with Picture Books*, Stroud, Thimble Press.

Bettelheim, B. and Zelan, K. (1982). *On Learning To Read: The Child's Fascination with Meaning*, London, Thames and Hudson.

Branston, P. and Provis, M. (1986). 'Children and parents', in CAPER, *Enjoying Reading*, London, Hodder and Stoughton.

Bruner, J. (1986). *Actual Minds, Possible Worlds*, Cambridge, Mass., Harvard Educational Press.

Burningham, J. (1974). *The Snow*, London, Jonathan Cape.

Butler, D. (1979). *Cushla and Her Books*, London, Hodder and Stoughton.

—(1980). *Babies Need Books*, Harmondsworth, Penguin.

—(1986). *Five to Eight*, London, Bodley Head.

CACE (1967). *Children and their Primary Schools*. The Report of the Central Advisory Council for England, Volume 1.

Carpenter, H. (1977). *J. R. R. Tolkien: A Biography*, London, Allen and Unwin.

Clark, M. (1970). *Reading Difficulties in Schools*, Harmondsworth, Penguin.

—(1976). *Young Fluent Readers*, London, Heinemann.

Clay, M. (1979). *Reading: The Patterning of Complex Behaviour*, London, Heinemann.

Davies, P. and Williams, P. (1974). *Aspects of Early Reading Growth*: A Longitudinal Study, Oxford, Blackwell.

DES (1967). *Children and their Primary Schools*; The Plowden Report, London, HMSO.

—(1975). *A Language for Life*, (The Bullock Report) London, HMSO.

—(1982). *Education 5 to 9: An Illustrative Survey of Eighty First Schools in England*, London, HMSO.

—(1984). *English 5–16*, London, HMSO.

—(1987). *Teaching Poetry in the Secondary School*, London, HMSO.

DES and the Welsh Office (1988a). *English for Ages 5–11*, London, HMSO.

—(1988b). *National Curriculum: Task Group on Assessment and Testing*, London, HMSO.

—(1988c). *Mathematics for Ages 5–16*, London, HMSO.

—(1988d). *Science for Ages 5–16*, London, HMSO.

Donaldson, M. (1978). *Children's Minds*, London, Fontana/Collins.

Downing, J. (1974). 'Some curious paradoxes in reading research' in *Reading*, 8, 2–10.

—(1978). 'How children think about reading' in J. Chapman, (ed.), *Reading: From Process to Practice*, Milton Keynes, Open University Press.

—(1985). 'The child's understanding of the functions and processes of communication' in M. Clark (ed.), *New Directions in Reading*, London, Falmer Press.

Esnouf, P. (1983). In *Parents in Partnership (Ideas for Involving Parents in School Reading Programmes)*, The Centre for the Teaching of Reading.

Francis, H. (1977). *Language in Teaching and Learning*, London, Allen & Unwin.

Fraser, E. (1959). *Home Environment and the School*, London, University of London Press.

Gesell, A. *et al.* (1977). *The Child from Five to Ten*, London, Harper and Row.

Goddard, N. (1974). *Literacy: Language Experience Approaches*, London, Macmillan.

Gollasch, F. (ed.) (1982). *Language and Literacy: The Collected Writings of Kenneth S. Goodman*, Vols 1, 2, London, Routledge and Kegan Paul.

Goodman, K. S. (1967). 'Reading: a psycholinguistic guessing game' in R. Wardhaugh, *Reading, a Linguistic Perspective*, New York, Harcourt, Brace and World Inc.

—(1973a). 'Miscues: windows on the reading process' in K. S. Goodman (ed.), *Miscue Analysis, Applications to Reading Instructions*, Urbana, Illinois, ERIC.

—(1973b). In R. Karlin, *Perspectives on Elementary Reading*, New York, Harcourt, Brace, Jovanovich.

—(1987). *What's Whole in Whole Language*, Leamington Spa, Scholastic.

Goodman, P. (1974). 'Minischools, a prescription for the reading programme', in I. Listes (ed.), *Deschooling*, Cambridge, Cambridge University Press.

Halliday, M. A. K. (1969). 'Relevant models of language', *Educational Review*, 22, 1, 26–37.

Harrison, C. (1979). 'Assessing the readability of school texts' in E. Lunzer and K. Gardner (eds), *The Effective Use of Reading*, London, Heinemann.

Heaney, S. (1980). *Preoccupations: Selected Prose 1968–79*, London, Faber.

Heath, S. Brice (1982). 'What no bedtime story means: narrative skills at home and at school', *Language in Society*, 11, 49–75.

—(1983). *Ways with Words*, Cambridge, Cambridge University Press.

Heeks, P. (1982). *Ways of Knowing: Information Books for 7 to 9 Year Olds*, Stroud, Thimble Press.

Holdaway, D. (1972). *Independence in Reading*, Sydney, Ashton Scholastic.

—(1979). *The Foundation of Literacy*, Sydney, Ashton Scholastic.

Hughes, J. M. (1975). *Reading and Reading Failures*, London, Evans.

ILEA (1983). *Stories in the multi-lingual primary classroom: Supporting Children's Learning of English as a Second Language*, London, ILEA Learning Resource Branch.

Keats, E. J. (1964). *Whistle for Willie*, Harmondsworth, Penguin in association with The Bodley Head.

Kent, N. and Davis, D. R. (1975). 'Discipline in the home and intellectual development', *British Journal of Medical Psychology*, 30, 27–33.

Kennedy, A. (1984). *The Psychology of Reading*, London, Methuen.

Kidman Cox, R. (1980). *Understanding Zoo Animals*, London, Usborne Publishing.

Kress, G. (1982). *Learning to Write*, London, Routledge and Kegan Paul.

Lavender, R. (1983). 'Children using information books', *Education 3–13*, 11, 1.

Lunzer, E. and Gardner, K. (1979). *The Effective Use of Reading*, London, Heinemann.
—(1984). *Learning from the Written Word*, Edinburgh, Oliver and Boyd.
Maddock, R. (1969). In A. Chambers *The Reluctant Reader*, Oxford, Pergamon.
Mark, J. (1978). *Thunder and Lightnings*, London, Puffin.
McKenzie, M. (1979). *Learning to Read and Reading*, London, ILEA.
—(ed.) (1985). 'Shared writing: apprenticeship in writing', *Language Matters*, London, ILEA Centre for Language in Education.
Meek, M. (1977). 'What is a horse?', *The School Librarian*, 25, 1.
—(1982). *Learning to Read*, London, Bodley Head.
—(1988). *How Texts Teach What Readers Learn*, Stroud, Thimble Press.
Moon, C. (1980). *Individualised Reading*, Reading, Centre for the Teaching of Reading, University of Reading.
—(1984a). 'The teaching of reading: where are we now?' (unpublished).
—(1984b). 'Recent developments in the teaching of reading' in *English in Education*, 18, 1, 20–6.
Moss, E. (1978). 'Storytelling' in C. Richards (ed.), *Education 3–13*, Nafferton Books.
National Association of Head Teachers (NAHT) (1988). *Home–School Contracts of Partnership*, W. Sussex, NAHT Publications.
Opie, I. and Opie, P. (1959). *The Lore and Language of School Children*, Oxford, Oxford University Press.
Paice, S. (1984). 'Reading to learn', *English in Education*, 18, 1, 3–8.
Perera, K. (1986). 'Some linguistic difficulties in school text-books' in B. Gillham (ed.), *The Language of School Subjects*, London, Heinemann Educational Books.
Reid, J. F. (1966). 'Learning to think about reading', *Educational Research*, 9, 56–62.
Richmond-Watson, Z. (1984). *The Use and Abuse of Animals*, London, Macdonald.
Richmond, J. (1985). *A Policy for Writing* (unpublished paper), National Writing Project, July 1985.
Schools Curriculum Development Committee (SCDC) (1988). *About Writing*, National Writing Project Newsletter, 8.
Skeels, H. (1966). 'Adult status of children with contrasting early life experiences: a follow-up study', Monographs of the Society for Research in Child Development, 31, 3.
Smith, F. (1971). *Understanding Reading*, London, Holt, Rinehart and Winston.
—(1978a). *Understanding Reading: A Psycholinguistic Analysis of Reading and Learning to Read*, London, Holt Rinehart and Winston.
—(1978b). *Reading*, Cambridge, Cambridge University Press.
—(1982a). *Writing and the Writer*, London, Heinemann Educational Books.
—(1982b). *Understanding Reading* London, Holt, Rinehart and Winston.
—(1985). *Reading* 2nd edn., Cambridge University Press.
Southgate, V., Arnold, H. and Johnston, S. (1981). *Extending Beginning Reading*, London, Heinemann.
Spencer, M. (1976). 'Stories are for telling', *English in Education'*, 10, 1, 16–23.
Stein, N. L. and Glenn, C. G. (1979). 'An analysis of story comprehension in elementary school children' in R. O. Freedle, *Discourse Processing: Multidisciplinary Perspectives*, Hillsdale, NJ, Ablex In.
Story Chest (1982). Leeds, Arnold Wheaton.
Tizard, B. and Hughes, M. (1982). *Young Children Learning*, London, Fontana.

van Lierop, M. (1985). 'Predisposing factors in early literacy: a case study' in M. Clark (ed.), *New Directions in Reading* (1985), London, Falmer Press.

Vygotsky, L. S. (1962). *Thought and Language*, Cambridge, Mass., MIT Press.

—(1983). 'School instruction and mental development' in M. Donaldson *et al.* (eds), *Early Childhood Development and Education: Readings in Psychology*, Oxford, Blackwell.

Wade, B. (1978). 'What a pity Richard can read', *Cambridge Journal of Education*, 8, 1, 52–6.

—(1984). *Story at Home and School, Educational Review*, Occasional Publication 10, University of Birmingham.

—(ed.) (1985). *Talking to Some Purpose, Educational Review*, Occasional Publication 12.

Warlow, A. and Meek. M. (eds) (1977). *The Cool Web*, London, Bodley Head.

Waterland, L. (1985). *Read With Me: An Apprenticeship Approach to Reading*, Stroud, Thimble Press.

Webb, K. (1979). *I like this poem*, Puffin.

Wells, G. (1981). *Learning Through Interaction*, Cambridge, Cambridge University Press.

—(1982). *Language, Learning and Education*, Bristol, Centre for the Study of Language and Communication, University of Bristol.

—(1987). *The Meaning Makers*, London, Hodder and Stoughton.

Whitehead, F., Capey, A. C. and Maddren, W. (1974). *Children's Reading Interests*, London, Schools Council.

Whitehead, F., Capey, A. C., Maddren, W. and Wellings, A. (1977). *Children and Their Books*, Basingstoke, Macmillan.

Wood, D., McMahon, L. and Cranstoun, Y. (1980). *Working with Under Fives*. Grant McIntyre.

Index